THE

PIRATE HANDBOOK

A ROGUE'S GUIDE TO PILLAGE, PLUNDER, CHAOS & CONQUEST

PAT CROCE

CHRONICLE BOOKS

SAN FRANCISCO

Library of Congress Cataloging-in-Publication Data
Croce, Pat.
The pirate handbook : a rogue's guide to pillage, plunder, chaos & conquest / Pat Croce.
p. cm.
ISBN 978-0-8118-7852-4 (hardcover)
1. Pirates—History. I. Title.
G535.C75 2011
910.4'5—dc22
2011005944

Manufactured in China

Designed by EMILY DUBIN

10 9 8 7 6 5 4 3 2 1

Chronicle Books
680 Second Street
San Francisco, California 94107
www.chroniclebooks.com

"There comes a time in every rightly constructed boy's life when he has a raging urge to go somewhere and dig for hidden treasure."

MARK TWAIN

TABLE OF CONTENTS

Pirate. Upon hearing this word, your mind should instantly conjure up fantastic images: swashbuckling rogues swinging from the rigging of tall ships, daggers firmly clenched between teeth. Wicked boarding axes and razor-sharp cutlasses clashing against one another again and again and again. Lean, tanned bodies slick with sweat and sea spray, fighting tooth and nail to the death. Thick clouds of black powder smoke blotting out the horizon as volley after volley of cannon fire from broadsides transforms wood into splinters and men into ghosts. Hordes of treasure—gleaming gold doubloons and silver pieces of eight, precious gemstones and ornate jewelry, priceless artifacts and rare antiquities—enough wealth to last a hundred lifetimes and justify the taking of a hundred lives. And then there are the names: Blackbeard, Captain Kidd, Black Bart, Thomas Tew, Anne Bonny, Henry Morgan— names that cause a tremor among the living, or bring a smile to the dead.

We are the last of our kind, and we don't take our profession lightly. In fact, I'd venture to say it's not a profession at all—it's a lifestyle. And if you choose to join our ranks you'd best come prepared.

Fightin', drinkin', gamblin', whorin'. . . What most consider vices, to be avoided like the plague, we consider fun, to be engaged in whenever possible. And engage in 'em we do, but only after prizes have been boarded and plundered, and the booty's been divided. There's no sense celebrating if there's nothing to celebrate about.

Now there are those who believe an honest day's work equals an honest day's pay. *Bilge!* That lily-livered mentality will bring you nothing but boredom, regret, and poverty. But pirating on the other hand, well matey, that's a life worth livin'.

It doesn't matter where you hail from, or if your bloodline is pauper or prince. Your reasons for sailing under the black flag—be it running from your past or 'cause you've had salt in your bones since you first sucked air—are yours and yours alone. So long as you sign the Articles and carry your weight, the brethren of the coast will embrace you with open arms.

Ah, the Articles. That's our code of conduct, spelling out the rights, duties, and powers for all aboard the ship, crewmen and officers alike. We wrote 'em together, we obey 'em together, until the day our hearts beat no more. Chores and responsibilities, leisure activities, sharing booty, arguments and disputes—the Articles cover it all. And make no mistake, the Articles leave no room for interpretation. The code is gospel, more important than the water we drink or the air we breathe.

So make your mark, put a fresh grind on your blade, and prepare yourself for exotic lands, amazing sights, and incredible adventures, all far beyond imagination. 'Tis a hard life you've chosen, one that may have lasted considerably longer had you remained at home. Then again, had you stayed put, you'd never have fulfilled your destiny and unleashed your pirate soul.

Welcome aboard!

The Pirate's Articles

I.   Every man shall have an equal vote in affairs of moment. He shall have an equal title to the fresh provisions or strong liquors at any time seized.

II.   The captain and quartermaster shall each receive two shares of a prize, the master gunner and boatswain, one and one half shares, all other officers one and one quarter, and private gentlemen of fortune one share each.

III.   Every man shall be called fairly in turn by the list on board of prizes. But if he defrauds the company to the value of even one dollar of plate, jewels, or money, he shall be marooned. If any man rob another he shall have his nose and ears slit, and be put ashore where he shall be sure to encounter hardships.

IV.   That Man that shall snap his Arms, or smoke Tobacco in the Hold, without a Cap to his Pipe, or carry a Candle lighted without a Lanthorn, shall receive Moses's Law (that is, 40 Stripes lacking one) on the bare Back.

V.   None shall game for money either with dice or cards on board ship.

VI.   Each man shall keep his piece, cutlass, and pistols at all times clean and ready for action.

VII. If any man shall offer to run away, or keep any Secret from the Company, he shall be marooned with one Bottle of Powder, one Bottle of Water, one small Arm, and Shot.

VIII. If at any time you meet with a prudent Woman, that Man that offers to meddle with her, without her Consent, shall suffer present Death.

IX. None shall strike another on board the ship, but every man's quarrel shall be ended onshore by sword or pistol.

X. Every man who shall become a cripple or lose a limb in the service shall have 800 pieces of eight from the common stock and for lesser hurts proportionately.

XI. The musicians shall have rest on the Sabbath Day only by right. On all other days by favor only.

IN WITNESS WHEREOF, THE PARTIES HAVE DULY EXECUTED THESE ARTICLES THE DATE AND YEAR LAST WRITTEN BELOW:

_____ _____

NAME AND DATE

ahoy!

CHAPTER
ONE

PREPARATIONS

&

PROVISIONS

"We are waiting for you with pleasure,
and we have powder and ball
with which to receive you."

HENRY MORGAN

**B**ecoming a sea devil is not a decision to be taken lightly. Countless perils await, many of which will send you to Davy Jones's locker long before your time. However, for those who throw caution to the wind, sign the Articles, and sail under the black flag, a life of action and adventure—and possibly great fortune—is sure to follow.

Still, before you cross the gangplank and come aboard, you'd be wise to equip yourself with the specialized accoutrements and requisite skills for your chosen career. Space is at a minimum—you're not captain yet, no private cabin in your immediate future; whatever you can pack into your duffel will have to suffice. Thus, you need to pack wisely—necessities not luxuries. Pirate ships are cramped enough. Besides, you'll find more than enough plunder aboard your first prize.

Proper clothing is your first priority. Layers are the key. Better to have 'em and not need 'em than need 'em and not have 'em. Add or subtract based on what Mother Nature throws at you.

At the bare minimum this means a sturdy pair of canvas pants, a loose-fitting cotton top (long sleeves are best for sun protection), and an overcoat that is both wind- and water-resistant. Add in appropriate undergarments and you've got a multiuse outfit that will get you just about anywhere.

When it comes to footwear, sailors don't have many choices. In some cases, there's no choice at all, especially if they've been press-ganged or conscripted (forced into service). For these poor souls, the British Navy hands out *slops*—simple canvas doublets, breeches, cotton waistcoats and drawers, stockings, linen shirts, knitted wool caps, and run-of-the-mill shoes. Not only don't these garments fit particularly well when dry but, when soaked with sweat or saltwater—which is often—wearing them is akin to punishment. Trying to perform arduous chores in a marine environment, or worse, engaging in life-or-death naval combat, while wearing clothes that are too tight, too loose, or uncomfortable to the point of distraction is at least a nuisance and at worst a serious handicap. For this reason, when the weather is warm, crewmen usually go about bare-chested. I recommend you do the same.

MOTLEY CREW

This term came about to describe the multicolored ensembles pirates wore, representing the wide varieties of clothing plundered from various sources throughout their voyages.

THE MORE FEROCIOUS YOU LOOK, THE LESS YOU HAVE TO FIGHT!

When pirates go into battle, they go loaded for bear. But some take their arsenal and imagery to another level. **BLACKBEARD** routinely wore a bandolier-like sling across his blood-red brocaded coat, which held a triple brace of pistols. A well-used cutlass and dagger were tucked into his belt. His long black beard was tied with ribbons, and his straggly black hair was interwoven with slow-burning cannon fuses that, when lit, cast a smoky haze around his head, making him appear like a demon direct from Hades. The very sight of him often caused enemies to surrender without a struggle rather than chance dancing with the devil.

[FIG. 1] BLACKBEARD

But fear not. The sooner you turn from merchant or naval service to piracy, the sooner you can amass a proper wardrobe. Canvas, cotton, silk, velvet—we pirates adorn ourselves in a vast array of fabrics and colors, accumulated from a wide variety of passengers (many of whom were wealthy) from all sorts of cultures and nationalities.

A word of caution: Function is far more valuable than form. If it's comfortable and serves its purpose, it will be preferred over the most lavish finery. But that doesn't mean we pirates don't have a sense of style. Quite the contrary. Clothes worn aboard the ship—for work and/or battle—differ significantly from what we wear ashore during our, shall we say, "leisure time pursuits." As such, any items of finery or fashion are usually reserved for our more pleasurable on-island activities. After all, we aren't called "gentlemen of fortune" for nothing.

This mentality applies to all but the captains, who are almost always regally (and in some cases flamboyantly) attired. From their colorful waistcoats and sashes to impressive tri-cornered hats (often festooned with exotic bird feathers) to an abundant adornment of gold and silvery jewelry, pirate captains have an image to uphold, and the lavishness of their wardrobe often correlates to how much respect they command. By far, the pirate most notorious for his impressive attire was Black Bart Roberts. A snazzy dresser, Roberts routinely went into battle wearing a crimson damask waistcoat and breeches, with a red feather in his cap, and a large diamond cross—plundered booty originally intended for the King of Portugal—hanging around his neck.

Not all pirate captains subscribe to the "image is everything" mindset, however. Some intentionally wear less-than-stellar outfits—simple waistcoats and long sea coats, for example—to pass themselves off as officers on a privateer or merchant ship in an effort to fool any watchful eyes peering through a prey ship's spyglass. Ah, there are some clever minds in our ranks.

TOOLS OF THE TRADE

Proper Pirate Attire

OVERSIZE GOLDEN HOOP EARRINGS
Pirates, especially some of the fancier, more flamboyant captains, can often be seen with large gold hoop earrings dangling from their lobes. Obvious signs of wealth and success, there is an added benefit—the pressure they apply to the lobes, especially the heavier earrings, helps modulate equilibrium and will ease or eliminate seasickness. And if you die penniless, you can always bribe your way into Fiddler's Green (sailor's paradise) with your last bit of jewelry.

THE INFAMOUS EYE PATCH · Pirates don't wear eye patches because it makes them look mean or cool. Fragments of gunpowder (from muskets or flintlocks) destroy innumerable eyes, as do flying slivers of sharp wood from cannonball strikes to the gunwales. And then there are all the shipboard combat injuries, whether due to pistol and musket balls or cutlass and dagger slashes and thrusts. But eye damage frequently occurs under less harrowing circumstances. Prolonged staring into the harsh sun while using a cross-staff (which spurred the development of the backstaff) can render an eye just as blind.

SCARVES AND SASHES · Besides being an obvious fashion statement, scarves and sashes have a wide variety of uses. They can conceal small pistols and daggers, or even act as slings or holders for those very same weapons. They can be ripped into wadding for the firing of flintlocks and muskets. And, if the battle goes against you, they can be used as bandages or tourniquets. What's more, long, loose pieces of cloth can also be used as weapons, both offensive and defensive. You can defend against dagger and cutlass strikes, catch or imprison limbs, choke and constrict, or tie to a heavy object and use as a flail. But make sure they are secured in such a fashion so as not to be a liability during work or battle.

ROGUE STRATEGY

How to Tie a Bandana

Whether being used to keep hair out of your face, keep the sun off your head, reduce your body temperature after being soaked in cold water, or simply make you look cool while swashbuckling, bandanas are invaluable.

1 START by stealing a square of fabric, ideally twenty-four inches square or larger.

2 LAY it flat.

3 FOLD in half to make a triangle.

4 POSITION longest edge against your forehead at a height of your choosing.

5 PULL side corners toward the back of your head and tie a single knot on top of the middle point. Bandana should be firmly tied but not uncomfortable.

6 ADJUST tightness by pulling on the bottom corner flap and tightening knot in back.

Pirate crewmen, however, can't afford to worry about how their ensembles look. They have important work to carry out—getting it done properly and efficiently trumps getting it half-done looking fashionable by a cannon shot.

Flexible, formfitting clothing is preferred, especially among men working in the rigging. Clothing too loose can become ensnared in the lines and, when you're working more than a hundred feet above the deck sans safety harness or catch net, accidents don't have happy endings. And from a battle perspective, loose clothing will give your opponents something to latch onto.

It's for this reason that long, loose hair should be tied in a ponytail or secured beneath a bandana. Straggly, unkempt hair can pose a problem for crewmen in myriad ways: continually falling in their eyes, becoming tangled in sail rigging, or providing a "gripping point" for enemies.

Footwear also poses a major predicament. When decks become slick with seawater or blood (or both), secure footing is hard to come by with many of the commonly worn shoes or boots. Going barefoot, however, provides superior traction in even some of the worst conditions. Climbing the rigging is also much easier to perform without shoes.

Going barefoot does have a downside, though. For one, prolonged exposure to cold water often leads to hypothermia. Also, a significant amount of body heat is lost from exposed feet. But even worse, on-deck obstructions, especially during battle (when razor-sharp wooden splinters or mayhem-causing caltrops (see p. 98) are routinely scattered about), will wreak havoc on your bare flesh. Yet, for many sailors, the decision to go barefoot is not theirs, as the vast majority of footwear will literally fall apart as soon as it's been exposed to tropical climates and seawater.

The next item in your duffel of paramount importance is a knife or dagger. Without question, the most important tool any man—especially a pirate—should own is a well-made blade. The variety of tasks one can perform with a good knife far surpasses that of any other tool, or even combination of tools, you can think of.

Ideally, the knife you choose will be able to handle every kind of daily duty. Additionally, it should be able to assist you in putting food on the table, as well as enable you to defend yourself from an attacker should the situation arise. And it should be comfortable to hold and use, more an extension of your hand than a secondary implement.

Relatively small in size, with a straight blade seldom longer than six inches, the dagger is predominantly a double-edged weapon designed for thrusting and puncturing. A hilt (a.k.a. crossbar) will prevent your hand from sliding forward onto the blade during use and is capable of deflecting or, depending on the design, trapping your opponent's blade during a fight. When not being used for enemy bloodletting (secondary to the cutlass, of course), daggers are perfect tools for all aspects of piratical life—from shipboard chores (slicing rope, repairing sails) to cutting food during meals. Daggers are often referred to as "flesh knives" or "fruit knives" in honor of the "skin" they are best at slicing.

Another worthwhile item to include in your duffel would be a length of rope. Even better, save room inside the duffel and simply wind the rope around it, unwinding it as needed. Aboard a sailing vessel you can never have too much rope. From sail rigging to mooring tethers to anchor lines to safety belays for climbing the mast to restraints for unruly prisoners, sooner or later that extra rope will come in handy. What kind and how much is entirely up to you, but a hundred-foot coil of quality hemp rope that does not fray easily or abrade when exposed to saltwater is a good place to start.

Another reason to add a length of rope to your duffel would be for knotting practice. Any seaman worth the salt in his bones should be a walking glossary of basic maritime knots. The more you know—and know well—the better. Practice makes perfect; sailors should be able to tie a variety of knots in their sleep, to better prepare them for extreme conditions.

Piratical Tattoos

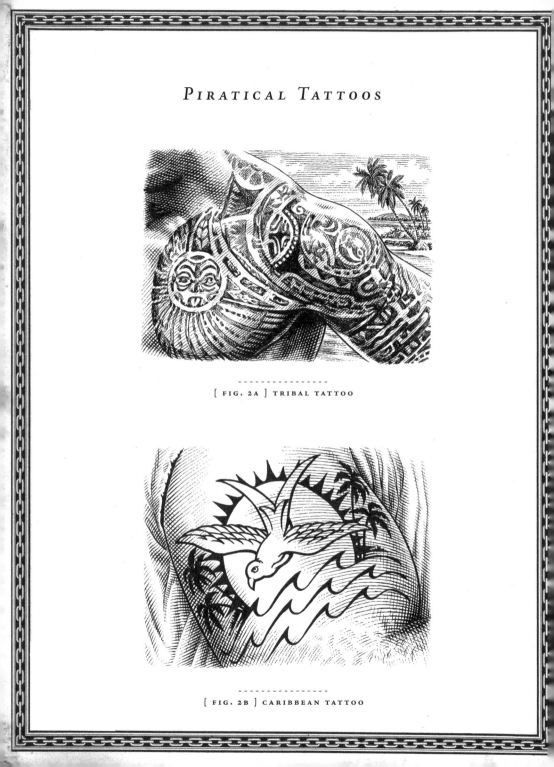

[FIG. 2A] TRIBAL TATTOO

[FIG. 2B] CARIBBEAN TATTOO

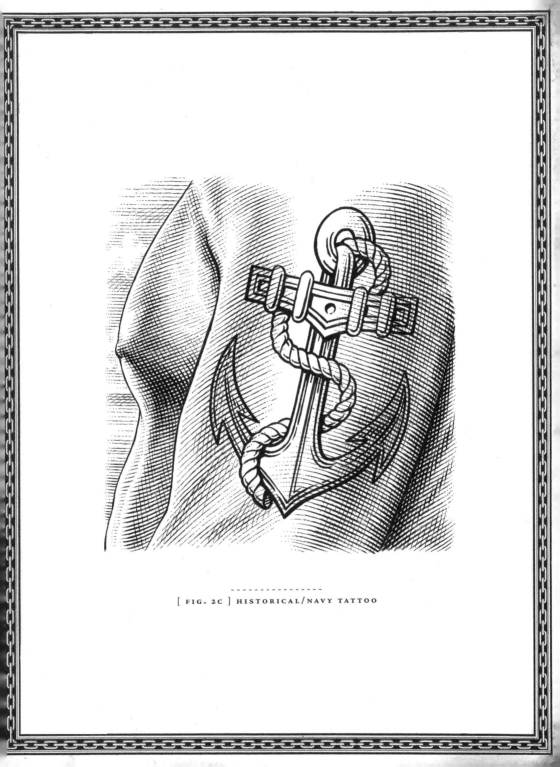

[FIG. 2C] HISTORICAL/NAVY TATTOO

The next item might not necessarily go in your duffel but, for most men going to sea, it's still a critical part of their kit. I'm talking about tattoos, ritual adornments, and good luck charms. Sailors are among the most superstitious men on the planet. Many among them believe their fate and fortune lies not in their skills and abilities but in the whims of the gods, be they Neptune, Poseidon, Yahweh, or Jesus. In an effort to influence those gods, or at least tip the scales in their favor, sailors take certain keepsakes with them wherever they go, in some cases even under their own skin, to ward off evil spirits or put them at ease.

Tattoos have been around for thousands of years. Descended from the word *tattau* (to hit or strike), every tattoo has a different meaning to its bearer. Regardless of what you decide to put on your skin canvas, you'd be wise to invest a little thought into it, for once it's on, it's not coming off so easily.

Just like with tattoos, all good luck charms and ritual adornments have different meanings to their possessors. But unlike tattoos, which are generally planned out before being acquired—even if only a few drunken seconds prior—charms and adornments can be acquired anywhere, at any time. Many of these trinkets and keepsakes come from plundered booty, reminding the new owner of the spoils of victory. Others, such as pieces of clothing, jewelry, locks of hair, or even droplets of blood in a glass vial, come from loved ones or enemies, and were taken specifically to commemorate an occasion or serve as a reminder.

Everything else in your duffel falls under the all-encompassing "personal items" category. And with space and weight at a premium, these should only be smallish items you need, not want. Consider a journal and quill to document your travels, a compact flask or flagon to keep your ration of rum, or a small set of eating utensils to make mealtimes that much more enjoyable.

Marking all personal items with your initials or, in the event you are looking to forge a new identity, carving or engraving a mark personal to you, is a wise course of action. This will come in handy in the event of a disagreement over ownership and go a long way toward assuring that the only crewman punished is the one who rightly deserves it.

Finally, you'll need a place to keep your valuables. After all, obtaining plunder is only half the piratical equation. Keeping it from being stolen is the other. While some so-called strongboxes are quite proficient at their charge, others will yield your treasured goods as easily as halved oysters give up their pearls. And unless you are captain of the vessel, it's doubtful you'll have the means to own a treasure chest.

Should you be so lucky, it goes without saying that the best treasure chests are those that cannot be easily opened. Whether this means a chest that is imposingly constructed, capable of withstanding serious abuse, or one that involves trickery and deceit—such as hidden keyholes—the simple fact remains: Only you should be able to open it.

Three-lock boxes have, you guessed it, three locks that must be unlatched with the proper keys before access is granted. Some have been known to incorporate booby traps (acid or black powder), thus destroying the contents—and often the unlucky opener, as well—if not unlocked properly.

Some of the most impressive examples of true treasure chests, of which very few remain, make use of a concealed keyhole, hidden in a sliding panel somewhere on the chest. The obvious front keyhole is merely a ruse and will undoubtedly cause anger and frustration after myriad unsuccessful opening attempts.

For carrying currency and coins on your person, some pirates use a concealable pouch—usually just two swatches of leather sewn together—hidden beneath a sash, tucked in their drawers, stashed in a boot, or hung from a cord around their necks.

But no matter what you pack into your duffel, and how thorough you think you've been, chances are you're going to forget something. But that's the beauty of being a pirate. When you really need something, all you have to do is be resourceful and create it or, better yet, find, subdue, and plunder it!

HAVANA

Twice a year the Spanish treasure fleet would make final repairs and provisions in Havana before setting sail for Seville. Meat, fish, poultry, fresh fruits and vegetables, able-bodied men, and the most important staple, rum, could all be sourced here.

JOLLY JACK TAR

While "Jack Tar" or "Jolly Jack Tar" refers to seamen of the Merchant or Royal Navy, it is also the methodology behind waterproofing. Seamen smear tar on their clothes to repel water. Some even plait their hair into pony-tails and smear them with tar, not to repel water but to prevent their hair from getting caught in the pulleys and other sailing rigs. Also, because hemp rope will rot and fall apart in wet and humid environments, many lines are also soaked in, or smeared with, tar.

The two women, *Anne Bonny* and *Mary Read*, prisoners at the bar, were then on board the said sloop, and wore men's jackets, and long trousers, and handkerchiefs tied about their heads: and that each of them had a machete and pistol in their hands, and cursed and swore at the men, to murder the deponent.

TESTIMONY OF DOROTHY THOMAS AT THE TRIAL OF THE TWO WOMEN PIRATES ON NOVEMBER 28, 1720

Hereupon, as soon as they were arrived at Gracias a Dios, they all put themselves into canoes, and entered the river, being 500 men; leaving only five or six persons in each ship, to keep them. They took no provisions, being persuaded they should find everywhere sufficient. But their hopes were found totally vain, not being grounded in God Almighty. For he ordain'd it so, that the Indians, aware of their coming, all fled, not leaving in their houses or plantations, which for the most part border on the sides of the river, any provisions or victuals. Hereby, in few days after they had quitted their ships, they were reduced to most extreme necessity and hunger.

In this laborious journey they were reduc'd to such extremity, that many of them devour'd their own shoes, the sheaths of their swords, knives, and other such things, being almost ravenous, and eager to meet some Indians, intending to sacrifice them to their teeth.

ALEXANDRE EXQUEMELIN,
Bucaniers of America (1684)

TREASURE CHEST

One of the only remaining treasure chests whose provenance involves a real pirate—in this case, **THOMAS TEW**—is on display at the St. Augustine Pirate & Treasure Museum. The chest weighs almost two hundred pounds empty, has a hidden lockbox inside, and the lid is secured with a dozen solid steel sliding bolts to keep it from being forced open by thieving hands.

[FIG. 3] BURIED TREASURE

heave ho!

CHAPTER
TWO

BATTEN DOWN
THE
HATCHES

*"It was such dogs as he that
put men on pyrating."*

—

JOHN PHILLIPS

Pirates are masters of the ocean. Because the ocean is where we choose to make our living, we have to be. Naturally, we bring galleon-loads of skill and passion to the craft. Basically, if it floats, we can sail it—and sail it well. Many pirates begin their sea-faring lives as privateers, or are pressed into service by their country's navy, so when they finally sail under the black flag, they already have years of experience under their belts and are beyond salty.

To properly operate a pirate ship, such as Henry Every's *Fancy* or Blackbeard's *Queen Anne's Revenge*, takes some learning. Landlubbers were not allowed to do more than the most menial tasks until they proved themselves worthy of greater responsibility. Sailors began their maritime careers on the bottom rung of the ladder, learning every chore and task along the way, hands-on, before moving up.

The first step in working on any sailing vessel, especially a tall ship, is to understand the rigging, of which there are two basic categories: *standing rigging* and *running rigging.*

Standing rigging consists of the structural supports for the masts and the sails. As its name implies, this equipment is almost always fixed in place, although on some of the larger, more involved vessels it can be adjusted slightly. Running rigging consists of all the ropes (lines) used to control the sails. Without the running rigging, sailors would have virtually no control of their vessels. That's why slicing the rigging during shipboard combat is just as effective as toppling the mast or tearing holes in the sails.

As soon as *sprogs* (newbie sailors) learn the components of the ship beneath them—which has to happen posthaste, or else!—they can participate in the operation of the vessel. And it all starts with the unfurling (opening) of the sails and getting the ship underway.

One thing all pirates must be proficient at is tying knots. Not just any knots, mind you, but specific knots for specific purposes and situations. On sailing vessels, lines are everywhere and, sooner or later, knots will be needed, no matter what chore you've been assigned. All pirates worth the rum in their veins can tie a variety of knots in their sleep or dead drunk.

TOOLS OF THE TRADE

STANDING RIGGING

HEADSTAY/FORESTAY, BACKSTAY, SIDESTAY/ SHROUDS: High-tension wires supporting the mast, connected to the hull at various points. They also provide a place for the jib sail to attach.

RUNNING RIGGING

HALYARD: A line used to hoist the sail into position, halyard descended from the phrase "to haul yards."

MAINSHEET: A line attached to the boom used to control the mainsail.

JIB SHEET: A line attached to the clew (free corner) of a jib sail.

TOPPING LIFT: A line that supports the boom when the sail is lowered.

TYPES OF SAILS

MAINSAIL: A ship's primary wind-catcher and its main source of power, attached to the mast and boom.

JIB: A triangular staysail fixed ahead of the foremast.

JENNY/GENOA SAIL: Originally called an *overlapping jib*, the jenny is a larger jib that will partially overlap the mainsail.

SPINNAKER: Balloon-like sails used when sailing downwind, also called *kites* or *chutes*.

[FIG. 4] SAILS

Know Your Knots

ANCHOR HITCH · Best used when tension on the line is fluctuating, such as with an anchor.

1 With tag end of the rope, make one or two round turns around the object.

2 Pass tag end around standing part of rope.

3 Pass tag end under the turns.

4 Tighten.

[FIG. 5A] ANCHOR HITCH

BOWLINE · One of the most versatile knots, bowlines can be used for just about anything.

1 Tag end of the rope is considered the "rabbit," standing part is the "tree," and first loop is the "hole."

2 Form two loops.

3 Put tag end through first loop. Rabbit comes out of the hole.

4 Rabbit goes around the tree.

5 Rabbit goes back down the hole.

6 Cinch tight.

[FIG. 5B] BOWLINE

CLOVE HITCH · Simple and fast to tie, clove hitches are used to secure rope to an object.

1 Pass tag end of rope around object and cross over.

2 Do another turn, then pass tag end beneath second turn and pull it through.

3 Cinch tight.

[FIG. 5C] CLOVE HITCH

FIGURE EIGHT · Essentially just a stopper knot, you will often find figure eights at the end of jib sheets.

1 Loop tag end over standing part of rope.

2 Loop under standing part.

3 Pass tag end over first part of first loop.

4 Pass through loop and cinch tight.

[FIG. 5D] FIGURE EIGHT

ROLLING HITCH · Extremely versatile, rolling hitches can be adjusted and tied under tension.

1 Make a round turn around the line you wish to exert pressure along, going in the direction of the strain.

2 Make a second turn in the same direction.

3 Pass line in front and away from strain.

4 Make a turn, then pass tag end between standing part of the line and the other line.

5 Cinch tight.

[FIG. 5E] ROLLING HITCH

SHEET BEND · Sheet bends are ideal for quickly attaching two lines (of similar diameter) together.

1 Make a loop in one of the lines.

2 Put tag end of second line through the loop, starting from below loop.

3 Pass tag end of second line behind standing part of first line.

4 Pass tag end over and through loop.

5 Cinch tight.

[FIG. 5F] SHEET BEND

As their name implies, sailing ships are hugely dependent on the wind. The sails capture the wind, harnessing it for power. However, pirates aren't content to go wherever Mother Nature takes us. We have specific areas we need to get to, such as merchant shipping lanes where prizes can be hunted, conquered, and plundered, so knowing how to work the wind is crucial. This requires not only competency with the equipment but an ability to recognize, and adjust to, ever-changing conditions, both with wind and sea. Those who are able to perform rise through the ranks. Those who can't best look for another line of work—quickly!—or pray God have mercy on your soul, for we'll have no use for ya'.

Tacking is a sailing ship's alignment with the wind. When the wind is to the right (starboard), the ship is on a *starboard tack*. When the wind is to the left (port), the ship is on a *port tack*. Because wind blows in varying directions, at varying strengths, for varying lengths of time, captains have to order myriad tacking maneuvers, often at a moment's notice, over the course of each journey to reach the intended destination. Captains who fail at this endeavor are often replaced at the first sign of incompetence— but we'll not speak of mutiny here. Foul words such as those should never see print.

Working the helm (a.k.a. steering the ship) is just as important as understanding the wind and tacking maneuvers. Avoiding reefs, shoals and sandbars; maintaining the keel in deep water; keeping the wind at your back; and being able to outmaneuver your prey, as well as your enemies, are all skills helmsmen have to master, otherwise the ship—and the entire crew with it—are doomed.

Because the seas are expansive and filled with peril, experienced navigators are crucial. Oftentimes the most successful pirate captains are the ones who can master all the elements of sailing themselves—from simple techniques (anchoring) to the more complicated aspects of seamanship (surviving severe storms and hurricanes)—rather than just recruit the necessary crewmen to do the job. 'Tis why only a small fraction of our ranks become legends while the rest become nothing more than fleeting memories that fade over time.

BATTEN DOWN THE HATCHES

Originating in the navy, where it meant preparing for a storm by fastening down strips of wood (battens) over hatches/openings and canvas over doorways, it soon became synonymous with preparing for trouble.

PRIVATEER

Private person or warship authorized by a queen, king, or government (via a letter of marque) to attack and destroy or plunder the ships of their enemies.

SHIVER ME TIMBERS!

An expression of excitement or awe, the term has two origins. The first references a cannonball striking a ship's mast or gunwales, sending splinters of timber flying like shrapnel. These shards, when embedded in flesh, would often become infected, resulting in amputation or death. The second origin has to do with sailing in heavy seas, when ships are lifted up and pounded down so hard that the timber is said to shiver.

PRESSED INTO SERVICE

To seize and, ultimately, force someone to work or, in this case, crew aboard a ship. Sometimes this is called being "press-ganged." Also known as *conscription*.

A GIFT POUND OF SUGAR IS BETTER THAN A TON OF HARD-FOUGHT CANE.

In 1721, **BARTHOLOMEW "BLACK BART" ROBERTS** came across a fleet of forty-two Portuguese merchant ships off the coast of Brazil. Instead of battling the entire fleet, Roberts singled out the ship he believed to be the best source of both booty and information. After skillfully navigating his way to her, Roberts commandeered the ship and forced its captain to tell him which ship in the fleet held the greatest treasure. Armed with that knowledge, Black Bart successfully attacked the 40-gun merchant ship the captain named and plundered a huge cache of booty.

ROGUE STRATEGY

Measuring Speed Using a Chip Log

Used to estimate a ship's speed, a *chip log* (a.k.a. *speed log*) is one of the oldest navigation devices. It consists of a wooden board attached to a line (*log-line*) with knots evenly spaced along its length, which is then dropped over the ship's stern (rear).

1 **CUT** a board into a circle twelve inches in diameter.

2 **CUT** out one-quarter of the circle. This is the *drogue*.

3 **ATTACH** log-line to drogue by way of a *bridle*: three lines connected to the vertex and to the two ends of the quadrant's arc. Amount of line needed depends on estimated top speed of your ship. The faster the ship, the more line you'll need.

4 **TIE** knots on the line at precise intervals—23.3 feet apart.

5 **DROP** log-line-tied drogue off the stern and count the number of knots that run out (or past a specific point on the deck) in fifteen seconds.

Calibrate Depth with a Lead Line

Also called a *sounding line*, a *lead line* measures depth of water. The lead is attached to the end of a long, thin rope with knots tied every six feet (*fathom*).

1 Cast the lead out in front of the vessel.

2 As the vessel catches up with the lead and the line runs perpendicular from the deck to the seabed, mark the level on the lead line.

3 Leather indicators can also be tied to the knots at varying intervals to make identification easier for specific depths.

[FIG. 6] LEAD LINE OR CHIP LOG

THERE'S FAR MORE TREASURE ABOVE THE WAVES THAN BELOW 'EM!

After striking out in the "wrecking" trade (diving on sunken wrecks for cargo and treasure), **SAMUEL "BLACK SAM" BELLAMY** turned to piracy and hooked up with **CAPTAIN BENJAMIN HORNIGOLD.** They plundered many prizes before parting ways. The crew on Black Sam's ship, the three-hundred-ton, 28-gun *Wyddah*, quickly elected him captain and went on to enjoy great piratical success under his leadership until hurricane winds and forty-foot seas swallowed the *Wyddah* and most of its crew off the coast of Cape Cod in 1717.

GUTS AND SMARTS APPLY TO LAD OR LASS.

After avenging her husband's death and protecting the castle named in his honor (Cock Castle, circa late sixteenth century), **GRACE O'MALLEY** turned to piracy and led plundering raids twenty vessels strong against innumerable ships traipsing along the west coast of Ireland. Eventually, Captain O'Malley received a pardon directly from Queen Elizabeth I in exchange for promising to fight the queen's enemies.

OCRACOKE ISLAND—
BLACKBEARD'S HIDEOUT

On November 21, 1718, LIEUTENANT ROBERT MAYNARD
weighed anchor and inched his two naval sloops—*Ranger*
and *Jane*—toward Ocracoke Island, off the North Carolina
coast. The Royal Navy had discovered that Blackbeard's
ship, *Adventure*, was anchored in the interior waters of
Pamlico Sound. This was a great location for Blackbeard's
hideout due to the sheer difficulty of navigating through
the many shoals and sandbars without grounding the vessel, which would undoubtedly yield a savage attack from
Blackbeard. To avoid this consequence, Maynard hired
two local pilots to guide his attack. The end result saw
Blackbeard's decapitated head hanging from Maynard's
ship's bowsprit.

[FIG. 7] BLACKBEARD'S DEMISE

ROGUE STRATEGY

Dropping Anchor

BAHAMIAN MOOR

If persistent current shifts are a problem in your chosen mooring area, the Bahamian Moor technique should work.

1 Drop one anchor upstream.

2 Drop another anchor downstream.

3 As your vessel shifts 180 degrees with the current, the two anchors alternate acting as the *riding anchor* (under tension up-current) and *lee anchor* (no tension down-current), with the boat always pointing bow up.

DUAL ANCHOR MOORING

When shifting winds are the problem, a dual anchor mooring is often the best remedy.

1 Set two anchors on windward side, approximately 45 to 60 degrees apart.

2 Anchor lines should form a V with boat centered at their crux.

3 To accomplish in light wind, drop your first anchor, then travel the length of that anchor's line across the wind at a right angle and drop your second anchor.

4 To accomplish in heavy wind, drop the first anchor, then travel at a 45-degree angle upwind and drop your second anchor abreast with the first. Allow your craft to drift back between the two anchors and adjust the mooring lines accordingly.

HAMMERLOCK MOORING

When experiencing heavy weather, a hammerlock mooring is extremely safe.

1 Anchor your boat as you normally would.

2 Drop second anchor on a short line directly off the bow.

3 Primary anchor will bear the majority of the load, but second anchor will steady the craft.

4 Under heavy wind, secondary anchor will most likely be dragged to a new position (a.k.a. *drudging*); drudging is the intentional dragging of an anchor to reduce movement.

Having fill'd our water, cut our wood, and got our ship in a sailing posture, while the blustering hard winds lasted, we took the first opportunity of settled gale to sail towards Manila. Accordingly June the 14th, 1687, we loosed from Pulo Condore, with the wind at S.W. fair weather at a brisk gale. The Pepper Junk bound to Siam remained there, waiting for an easterly wind; but one of his men, a kind of bastard Portuguese, came aboard our ship, and was entertained for the sake of his knowledge in several languages of these countries.

We were now afraid lest the currents might deceive us, and carry us on the shoals of Pracel, which were near us, a little to the N.W. but we passed on to the eastward, without seeing any sign of them; yet we were kept much to the northward of our intended course: and the easterly winds still continuing, we despaired of getting to Manila; and therefore began to project some new design; and the result was, to visit the island Prata, about the Lat. of 20 deg. 40 min. North.

WILLIAM DAMPIER,
A New Voyage Around the World (**1697**)

starboard!

CHAPTER
THREE

LIFE ABOARD

"A merry life and a short one
shall be my motto."

BLACK BART ROBERTS

T The pirate ship is the center of our existence. Aside from occasional shore excursions, work, play, and everything in between takes place aboard the ship.

To assure that all goes smoothly, a true democracy must exist. Color, class, and creed are all non-factors—every pirate is a free man and shares in all successes fairly. In fact, pirate ships are far more democratic than they're routinely given credit for; by comparison, life aboard the ship is a much fairer existence than on a merchant or Royal Navy vessel. By signing the Articles, you go on account and are given all the rights and privileges that your mates enjoy, ensuring that you are an "equal among equals." For example, a pirate captain, regardless of his heritage or past exploits, is voted into office by a majority vote. Every ship's Articles establish the terms by which booty is distributed. Most Articles decree that any man seriously injured in battle, to the point that a limb is lost or requires amputating, will receive an additional share of the plunder (if not more), proving that there truly is honor among thieves.

Each pirate also has the opportunity to distinguish himself and be promoted accordingly to a ship's officer, all the while reserving the right to leave the "life of fortune" at a time of his own choosing. This is the polar opposite of the British Royal Navy's class-based system, whereby crewmen receive no money, no title, no connections, few (if any) liberties, and, of course, no possibility of ever attaining an officer's rank.

Our democratic process applies to booty as well. All plunder is distributed by a fair system that provides slightly more for the captain and others in "management" or skilled positions, and equal shares for the rest.

Leading the so-called "management team" is the captain. Like the Pirate Mentors detailed throughout this book, this position requires heaping mounds of courage, jack-of-all-trades knowledge, ruthlessness, seafaring skills (navigation chief among them), and a whole lot of luck to lead a crew of rough-and-tumble, desperate, and hard-core men such as we to

In the Commonwealth of Pyrates, he who goes the greatest length of wickedness, is looked upon with a kind of envy amongst them, as a person of a more extraordinary gallantry, and is thereby entitled to be distinguished by some post, and if such a one has but courage, he must certainly be a great man. The Hero of whom we are writing, **Black-beard**, aimed at making his men believe he was a Devil incarnate. For being one day at sea, and a little flushed with drink, he says: "Come, let us make a Hell of our own, and try how long we can bear it." Accordingly he, with two or three others, went down into the hold, and closing up all the hatches, filled several pots full of brimstone, and other combustible matter, and set it on fire, and so continued till they were almost suffocated, when some of the men cried out for air. At length he opened the hatches, not a little pleased that he held out the longest.

CAPTAIN CHARLES JOHNSON,
A General History of the Pyrates (1726)

a life of rum, riches, and romance. The pirate captain needs to be "pistol-proof"—that is, an expert at ship handling, crew control, and naval warfare. He must also exude confidence and exert strong leadership whenever he's in the crew's presence, all the while keeping the men content and in good spirits. Captaining a pirate ship is like walking a tightrope over a pit of vipers—just one slip and he can go from reaping the rewards of countless treasures, to being marooned on a deserted island, finding himself impaled on a cutlass, or gargling on the barrel of a loaded flintlock.

Since many pirates have suffered severe abuse while crewing under tyrannical captains in the merchant service and/or the British Royal Navy—many crewmen are pressed into service against their will—we are, as a result, not a trusting lot and want to ensure that our rights are protected at all times. By signing the Articles, we effectively split the ship's command between the captain and the quartermaster, a sort of "checks and balances" system.

Similarly, the captain can also be voted out if a majority of the crew is dissatisfied with his performance. The only time a pirate captain has absolute, unequivocal authority is when the ship is engaged in battle. In those instances, too many cooks don't just spoil the soup—they get men killed! But as soon as the fighting's done, the captain is returned to being "first among equals" and the democracy resumes.

Other key roles aboard pirate ships include the elected position of the quartermaster, the appointed position of the sailing master, and the earned and highly respected post of the navigator.

The quartermaster has the authority to adjudicate any and all differences between captain and crew. His essential duties include maintaining order among the crew, meting out justice when required, overseeing the distribution of sustenance, and selecting and distributing the plunder from a captured prize. Oftentimes, the quartermaster will become the captain of a captured ship and will either sail the newly acquired vessel solo or in consort with the primary pirate vessel.

As one would expect, the sailing master's chief responsibility is to oversee the navigation of the ship and to keep the sails properly trimmed at all times. And the navigator is tasked with making sure the journey through the expansive seas, ever-treacherous river waterways, and uncharted shallow shoals does not result in becoming lost at sea, wrecked on a reef, or captured by the authorities or pirate-hunters.

Another vital role on pirate vessels is the position of gunner. The success of every encounter with a treasured merchant ship, Spanish galleon, or hated Royal Navy warship all boils down to one thing: superior firepower. The most powerfully armed and passionately engaged ship and crew will usually win the day. It is the gunner's job to keep the cannons, ordnance, weapons, and crew in top-notch fighting shape at all times, regardless of the conditions at sea or, much more important, aboard the ship itself.

Other key members of a pirate crew, for obvious reasons, are the "sea artists"—specialized positions that include the boatswain, cooper, carpenter, and surgeon. In many cases, the carpenter and surgeon are one in the same; scarily, they use the same tools! Pirates who are so severely wounded in battle that they are no longer able to fight often become sailmakers or cooks so that they can remain on account and continue sharing in the plunder of prizes.

Not as obvious but equally vital to the crew's overall mental health is the ship's musician. This talented ruffian brings levity and merriment to the monotony and boredom of extended time at sea. And in battle, his music is used to motivate the crew to a fevered frenzy, not to mention scare the living daylights out of the prey's crew.

Unfortunately, living conditions for the crew of most pirate ships are atrocious, and that's putting it mildly. Below decks is a dark, damp, and dreary environment, reeking with the combined stench of accumulated bilge water, unwashed bodies, and rotting meat and fish. Although meat is generally salted and preserved in barrels, it often goes rotten before the crew has a chance to enjoy their stores. The water smells awful and the

SHIFT TIME

- Like military or merchant vessels, the custom aboard pirate ships is to divide shipboard duties into regular "watches," each lasting four hours.

- Time is determined by sandglass, turned (restarted) every half hour.

- A ship's bell sounds with each turn, beginning with one stroke half an hour after midnight, and adding an extra stroke every half hour after that.

- Watches are changed every eight bells—4:00, 8:00, and 12:00.

COOPER (A.K.A. BARREL-MAKER)

Because virtually all food and drink (especially freshwater) is stored inside wooden casks, no pirate venture can be successful without even a modestly capable cooper.

BOATSWAIN

Also known as the bosun, bo'sun or bos'n, the boatswain is the supervisor of the other deck-working crewmen.

[FIG. 8] BARREL-MAKERS

biscuits quickly become infested with ugly black-headed weevil maggots. Stormy weather and leaks in the weed-infested hull will send seawater sloshing down the hatchways, causing the bilges to constantly fill with foul, muck-laden water.

The customary drill on pirate vessels is to fumigate the below decks with pans of brimstone or burning pitch, but nothing can prevent the permeating stink, ungodly filth, and rampant infestation of crawling and scurrying creatures that accumulates during long months at sea. Joining the vile party are the unending deluge of refuse particles, food morsels, rum spillages, and animal feces that collect in the bottom of the ship's hull, becoming a breeding ground for rats, cockroaches, countless other night critters, and a wide range of health-squelching bacteria. So if you're squeamish about such things, I suggest you seek "employment" elsewhere.

All sailors on the high seas are well aware of the unpleasantries and perils of life below decks. And because pirate ships normally carry a crew three to four times larger than merchant ships, this large company—while great for battle—results in an even more cramped and volatile environment. Sleeping side by side on the steerage floor, or on tightly packed hammocks swaying from the rafters in one continuous motion, is the norm.

Although there is always work to be done aboard a pirate ship, we still enjoy plenty of leisure time—too much, in some cases, as there are long periods of boredom between the action and excitement of sighting a prize's sails. Crewmen occupy their "downtime" with music, boarding drills, and games of cards and dice (although gambling aboard most pirate vessels is strictly prohibited—and set forth in the Articles—due to its disruptive effect on the confidence and cohesion of the crew). Nevertheless, many pirates with pocketfuls of fresh plunder prefer to risk the consequence of getting caught rather than squander an opportunity to increase their wealth.

Considering that pirates, in general, aren't sweet and cuddly—an errant glance among them can easily be the start of bloodshed—adherence to the Articles guarantees the peace. At the very least, it lets transgressors

[FIG. 9] CAT-O'-NINE-TAILS

CAT-O'-NINE-TAILS

This multi-tailed whipping device—a.k.a. "the cat"—
consists of nine tightly wound and knotted strands
of cord attached to a dowel of leather-bound wood.
Used for administering corporal punishment, it is
the source of the phrase: "Don't let the cat out of
the bag."

know what to expect should they decide to break the code. And when the Articles are breached, punishment is swift—and it ain't pretty!

Understand, the punishment isn't harsh because pirates crave violence and bloodshed—at least, not *all* of them—but because it must serve two purposes: to keep the rule-breaker from ever running afoul of the Articles again, and, more important, to serve as a visual (and visceral) lesson for the rest of the crew.

The most common punishment for breaking one of the ship's Articles is *flogging*—being lashed with a *cat-o'-nine-tails* across the bare back. As specified by the Articles, if one of the ship's commandments is broken, a vote is taken to mete out punishment. In keeping with the piratical democracy, even friends will vote against their mate if an Article has been infracted. To insure the captain doesn't simply flog men whenever he feels the urge, the flogging is only carried out by the quartermaster after a majority vote from the crew upholds the ruling, followed by the captain's order to commence. However, if the quartermaster feels the punishment doesn't fit the crime, he may call for another flogging vote—and possibly for the deposal of the captain!

Once guilt has been confirmed, the transgressor is secured either standing belly-up against the mast, bent over one of the big guns, or prone atop the deck grating. One dozen strokes is the usual sentence, administered by the quartermaster with the entire crew in attendance. In extreme cases the entire crew not only watch, they participate, delivering a stroke or two apiece. This is true judgment by your peers. Just imagine the damage to a man's body after 180 able-bodied men take their turn with the cat! To make matters worse, salt and/or brine is often introduced into the open wounds, intensifying the pain of the flogging, adding a horrific exclamation point to the penalty.

Whether a pirate's punishment involves a cat across the back or being clapped in irons in the ship's hold, he should consider himself truly lucky that he isn't marooned or, worse, keelhauled. These two fates are usually the end of the road; the latter is almost certainly a trip to Davy Jones's locker.

Making a Cat-O'-Nine-Tails

1. Start with a yard of rope (the thicker the better) and unravel half the length (eighteen inches), producing three separate "tails."

2. Uncurl each tail, leaving you with nine.

3. Add three equally spaced knots to the cat, one at the solid end of the rope, one at the junction where the nine tails begin forming the handle, and one between the two.

4. Braid the handle, wrap it in leather, or fit it to a piece of wood.

5. To make your cat even nastier, add small weights or shot to the tips of each tail.

6. Some particularly sinister pirates affix fishhooks to the tips of their cat's tails. Ouch!

Using a Cat-O'-Nine-Tails

1. Line up to the side of your target.

2. Swing away.

3. Note that the whip's ends will leave nasty welts, while the knots/weighted tips will leave awful bruises, often tearing the skin, as well.

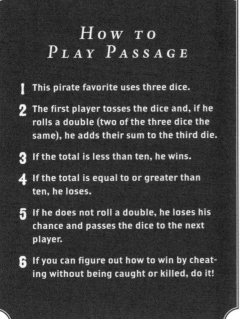

How to Play Passage

1. This pirate favorite uses three dice.

2. The first player tosses the dice and, if he rolls a double (two of the three dice the same), he adds their sum to the third die.

3. If the total is less than ten, he wins.

4. If the total is equal to or greater than ten, he loses.

5. If he does not roll a double, he loses his chance and passes the dice to the next player.

6. If you can figure out how to win by cheating without being caught or killed, do it!

Don't strike your captain!

Aboard **BARTHOLOMEW "BLACK BART" ROBERTS**'s *Royal Fortune*, when a drunken crewman, Thomas Jones, cursed Black Bart for killing another drunken crewmember, the enraged captain drew his sword and stabbed Jones. Jones did not take kindly to the attack; he threw Roberts over a cannon and beat him unmercifully. Following the fight, Black Bart had his quartermaster call for a vote. The crew voted unanimously to uphold the captain's honor and dignity. So when Jones's stab wound healed, he was tied to the mast and given two lashes with the cat by all 180 members of the crew.

THE PIRATE SONG

Virtually every major event or task aboard a pirate ship is accompanied by a song or chant: raising the anchor, raising the masthead, trimming the sails, pumping out bilge water, plundering a prize, celebrating a victory over an enemy, etc. The chanter (a.k.a. chantyman) sings the body and we pirates shout the chorus back:

- -

To the mast nail our flag, it is dark as the grave,
Or the death which it bears while it sweeps o'er the wave;
Let our deck clear for action, our guns be prepared;
Be the boarding-ax sharpened, the scimitar bared;
Set the canisters ready, and then bring to me,
For the last of my duties, the powder-room key.

It shall never be lowered, the black flag we bear;
If the sea be denied us, we sweep through the air.
Unshared have we left our last victory's prey;
It is mine to divide it, and yours to obey;
There are shawls that might suit a sultana's white neck,
And pearls that are fair as the arms they will deck.

There are flasks which, unseal them, the air will disclose
Diametta's fair summers, the home of the rose.
I claim not a portion: I ask but as mine
'Tis to drink to our victory—one cup of red wine.
Some fight, 'tis for riches—some fight, 'tis for fame:
The first I despise, and the last is a name.

I fight, 'tis for vengeance! I love to see flow,
At the stroke of my sabre, the life of my foe.
I strike for the memory of long-vanished years;
I only shed blood where another shed tears,
I come, as the lightning comes red from above,
O'er the race that I loathe, to the battle I love.

- -

[FIG. 10] SINGING PIRATES

Marooning is a drastic measure of punishment often reserved for cowardly conduct, 'such as deserting the ship during battle or defrauding fellow crewmen of their proper shares of plunder. To be made "governor of an island" entails being left on a deserted island with the bare minimum of supplies—usually just a flask of rum, a flintlock, some gunpowder, and one round of shot. Often that single round represents the fastest and least painful way off the island. Failure to drop the hammer on yourself almost always means a slow death by dehydration, starvation, or exposure to the elements.

Keelhauling involves binding the condemned man's hands and feet with rope, tossing him overboard, and hauling him from one side of the ship to the other, directly under the vessel's keel. This punishment is bad enough in itself, but then there are the secondary side effects to consider. Razor-sharp barnacles that cling to the ship's hull will turn the vessel into the world's largest cheese grater, scraping and tearing the skin, leaving the victim a raw and bloody mess. Or, if the keelhauling is done too deep, the penalized man might escape the perilous barnacles, only to receive virtually the same treatment from a coral reef. Oftentimes, only a shredded and bloodstained rope is pulled back onto the deck. Those who do return topside are usually just lifeless corpses, with drowning or shark attack to blame. But even the victims who are strong enough to survive the initial ordeal don't elude the Grim Reaper for long; the multiple infected wounds only delay the inevitable.

Forcing an Article-breaker to walk the plank isn't a usual punishment, despite many rumors to the contrary. Instead, we simply tie the miscreant to a dead body and chuck 'em both over the gunwales.

Another form of punishment involves tying the offender to the mast for any length of time and letting Mother Nature mete out justice. The time of year and the ship's location when the sentence is carried out have a lot to do with how well the victim will fare.

TIED TO THE MAST

A newspaper article from 1726, "The Tryal of Captain Jeane," provides a graphic account of how the cruel and sadistic **CAPTAIN JEANE** of Bristol tortured his eighteen-year-old cabin boy for stealing a mere dram of rum. After being whipped, pickled in brine, and then tied to the main mast for nine straight days with his arms and legs fully extended, Captain Jeane decided more punishment was necessary. So he untied the boy, laid him along the gangway, and trampled over him, back and forth, ultimately encouraging the entire crew to join him. Rather than join in the abuse, the men deposed Captain Jeane in the most serious manner possible—they hung him!

PORT ROYAL

Port Royal, on Jamaica's southern coast, was often referred to as "The Pirate Capital of the World." Located along shipping lanes between Spain and Panama—happy hunting grounds for prizes—it was perfectly situated for launching raids against Spanish settlements. Heralded for its debauchery, the city had at least one tavern or grog shop for every ten residents. Unfortunately, on June 7, 1692, the gods put an end to our Jamaican romps by hitting Port Royal with three powerful earthquakes and a devastating tsunami, wiping out two-thirds of the city in one fell swoop.

YOU CAN BEAT US BUT YOU'LL NEVER DEFEAT US.

Immediately following the destruction of the *Ranger* by the HMS *Swallow*, **CAPTAIN JAMES SKYRM**—who sailed in consort with **BLACK BART ROBERTS**—ordered their black flag thrown overboard so the Royal Navy could not display it in triumph.

BLACK BART ROBERTS'S
ARTICLES

from his ship, Royal Fortune

- -

I. Every man shall have an equal vote in affairs of moment. He shall have an equal title to the fresh provisions or strong liquors at any time seized.

II. Every man shall be called fairly in turn by the list on board of prizes. But if he defrauds the company to the value of even one dollar of plate, jewels, or money, he shall be marooned. If any man rob another he shall have his nose and ears slit, and be put ashore where he shall be sure to encounter hardships.

III. None shall game for money either with dice or cards.

IV. The lights and candles shall be put out at eight at night, and if any of the crew desire to drink after that hour they shall sit upon the open deck without lights.

V. Each man shall keep his piece, cutlass, and pistols at all times clean and ready for action.

VI. No boy or woman to be allowed amongst them. If any man shall be found seducing any of the latter sex and carrying her to sea in disguise he shall suffer death.

VII. He that shall desert the ship or his quarters in time of battle shall be punished by death or marooning.

VIII. None shall strike another on board the ship, but every man's quarrel shall be ended onshore by sword or pistol.

IX. No man shall talk of breaking up his way of living till each has a share of 1,000. Every man who shall become a cripple or lose a limb in the service shall have 800 pieces of eight from the common stock and for lesser hurts proportionately.

X. The captain and quartermaster shall each receive two shares of a prize, the master gunner and boatswain, one and one half shares, all other officers one and one quarter, and private gentlemen of fortune one share each.

XI. The musicians shall have rest on the Sabbath Day only by right. On all other days by favor only.

Captain John Phillips's
ARTICLES

from his ship, Revenge

I.   Every Man shall obey civil Command; the Captain shall have one full Share and a half of all Prizes; the Master, Carpenter, Boatswain, and Gunner shall have one Share and quarter.

II.   If any man shall offer to run away, or keep any Secret from the Company, he shall be marooned with one Bottle of Powder, one Bottle of Water, one small Arm, and Shot.

III.   If any Man shall steal any Thing in the Company, or game, to the Value of a Piece of Eight, he shall be marooned or shot.

IV.   If any time we shall meet another Marooner that Man shall sign his Articles without the Consent of our Company, shall suffer such Punishment as the Captain and Company shall think fit.

V.   That Man that shall strike another whilst these Articles are in force, shall receive Moses's Law (that is, 40 Stripes lacking one) on the bare Back.

VI.   That Man that shall snap his Arms, or smoke Tobacco in the Hold, without a Cap to his Pipe, or carry a Candle lighted without a Lanthorn, shall suffer the same Punishment as in the former Article.

VII.   That Man shall not keep his Arms clean, fit for an Engagement, or neglect his Business, shall be cut off from his Share, and suffer such other Punishment as the Captain and the Company shall think fit.

VIII.   If any Man shall lose a Joint in time of an Engagement, he shall have 400 Pieces of Eight; if a Limb, 800.

IX.   If at any time you meet with a prudent Woman, that Man that offers to meddle with her, without her Consent, shall suffer present Death.

Lesser offenses, such as fighting between crewmembers, are normally settled on land, where the antagonists are instructed to settle their differences via duel—pistols at ten paces (see Black Bart's Article VIII). Conflicts among crewmen are not seen just as a morale buster but as a display of complete and utter disrespect for the captain and his officers. Simply put, any and all shipboard disagreements between pirates would be settled at first landfall, either by pistol or sword (or both, depending on the result of the first volley). And so, to the duel we go:

- Adversaries begin the duel back-to-back, pistols cocked and ready.

- At the quartermaster's call ("One!"), dueling pirates take one pace forward.

- Forward progression continues with the next pace occurring at the exact moment of the quartermaster's decree.

- Some combatants hold their pistols tight to their bodies, muzzles pointed skyward, elbows at a right angle. *Fools!*

- To win the duel, have your pistol already aimed—as much as possible—thereby requiring less movement, and allowing for a faster shooting action, when the final pace is announced.

- Rather than having to spin, lower the weapon, aim, and fire, keeping your pistol aimed from the start (waist high is ideal, as the ball will rise en route to its target) will tip the scales in your favor.

- Becoming a smaller target—by crouching, for instance—while taking the paces is a sensible approach to not only winning the duel but surviving it. By "becoming small," duelers have a better chance of steadying their weapons, improving their aim and the likelihood of a hit on their opponent.

- Looking cool and/or brave is immaterial; someone is going to suffer pain, and, if you want it to be the other guy, anything you can do to tip the scales in your favor is worth trying.

- Don't wait for the call of "Ten!" to turn and fire. Instead, after the ninth pace, take a breath, turn, and fire.

- When it comes to gunfights and duels, there are no second chances. You're a pirate. If you have to cheat to win (and live), so be it!

What could be considered a form of punishment—but is actually a vital role aboard the ship—is being selected to man the crow's nest as "lookout." This duty requires carefully ascending to the top of the mainmast (often higher than a hundred feet above the deck), climbing into the crow's nest, and keeping a spyglass focused for sails (both enemies and prizes) on the horizon. The lookout is the ship's only early-warning mechanism, and the fate of the entire vessel often falls squarely on his shoulders—or more accurately, his eyes. But beyond the importance of the duty, there are the rigors that go with the territory. Even the most hardened sea dog will regularly suffer severe seasickness courtesy of the crow's nest's extreme height off the main deck, which amplifies its sway mightily on even the calmest of seas. And during severe weather conditions and high seas—forget it! Definitely not a place you want to relax with a mug of grog.

But despite the gruesome living conditions, strict codes of conduct, brutal nature of the "jobs," and the relatively short life spans, life aboard a pirate ship is the most exotic and romantic existence you can possibly experience.

From hence they resolved on a cruise between Cape Meise and Cape Nicholas, where they spent some time, without seeing or speaking with any vessel, till the latter end of November. Then they fell upon a ship, which 'twas expected would have struck soon as their black colours were hoisted; but instead of that, she discharged a broadside upon the Pyrate, and hoisted colours, which showed her to be a French Man of War. **Captain Charles Vane** desired to have nothing further to say to her, but trimm'd his sails, and stood away from the French man. But Monsieur, having a mind to be better informed who he was, set all his sails, and crowded after him. During this chase, the pyrates were divided in their resolutions what to do: Vane, the captain, was for making off as fast as he could, alleging the Man of War was too strong to cope with. But one **Jack Rackam**, who was an officer, that had a kind of check upon the captain, rose up in defense of a contrary opinion, saying "That tho' she had more guns, and a greater weight of metal, they might board her, and then the best Boys would carry the day." Rackam was well seconded, and the majority was for boarding; but Vane urged, "That it was too rash and desperate an enterprise, the Man of War appearing to be twice their force." The mate, one **Robert Deal**, was of Vane's opinion, as were about fifteen more, and all the rest joined with Rackam, the Quarter-Master. At length the captain made use of his power to determine this dispute, which, in these cases, is absolute and uncontrollable, by their own laws, viz. in fighting, chasing, or being chased; in all other matters whatsoever, he is governed by a majority. So the brigantine having the heels, as they term it, of the French man, she came clear off.

But the next day, the captain's behavior was obliged to stand the test of a vote, and a resolution passed against his honour and dignity, branding him with the name of coward, deposing him of the command, and turning him out of the company, with marks of infamy; and, with him, went all those who did not vote for boarding the French Man of War.

CAPTAIN CHARLES JOHNSON,
A General History of the Pyrates (1726)

scurvy!

CHAPTER
FOUR

GRUB
&
GROG

"Such a day; rum all out. Our company somewhat sober; a damned confusion amongst us! Rogues a-plotting. Talk of separation. So I looked sharp for a prize [and] took one with a great deal of liquor aboard. So kept the company hot, damned hot, then all things went well again."

—

BLACKBEARD

Pillaging and plundering requires energy—lots of it—so when it comes to food and drink, we pirates can't afford to be picky. This means choking down some things that would make a billy goat vomit. But since necessity is the mother of invention, this caused us to create some interesting foodstuff combinations, many of which will transform gastronomic horror shows into a feast fit for a king—a *pirate king*, that is!

Food preservation is a big problem on any ship, pirate ships included. Food items tend to spoil, rot, and mold over rather quickly, especially considering the humidity and salt air. The fresh meats, fruits, vegetables, and cheeses at the start of the voyage last about a week—if the crew is lucky. *Cackle fruit* can be had, provided the chickens have food. But once they stop laying eggs—or die—the birds go into the pot. Ditto for cows and fresh milk. Once the cow's food supply is exhausted, fresh meat finds its way onto the menu.

The rest of the food items have to be specially prepared to last and not go rancid. This usually means pickling or salting. Before long, bread is crawling with weevils, so *hardtack biscuits*—which last for an entire year—are a popular alternative, although some liken them to "digestible leather." Still, when a stomach is empty and grumbling, they hit the spot.

A good cook is worth his weight in gold, for a well-fed pirate is a happy pirate, and that means no mutinies for the captain and his officers to worry about. Experienced cooks are well versed in the use of exotic spices commonly found throughout the Caribbean island nations and, by relying on traditional native cooking methods, are capable of turning food items long past their prime into dishes that are not only edible but delicious.

Of course, depending on the conditions, location of the vessel, and success at finding prey, there are times when the pickings are beyond slim, which is just one of the reasons you don't see many so-called pets aboard a pirate ship. Colorful and often talkative shoulder-perched parrots won't last very long on a vessel full of starving pirates; undoubtedly, the captain would be the first to devour his companion bird.

BOUCAN

Meat prepared in a barbecue-like manner. It's where the term *buccaneer* derives from.

CACKLE FRUIT

Chicken eggs.

KILL-DEVIL

A potent combination of rum with a little gunpowder sprinkled on it.

SCURVY

A nasty disease resulting from a vitamin C deficiency, scurvy leads to the formation of spots on the skin, bleeding gums, and loss of teeth, and can be fatal if not treated. To avoid contracting scurvy, drink juice or eat fruit high in vitamin C (oranges, grapefruits, lemons, limes, kiwis, and strawberries).

BACCHANAL

A riotous, drunken party. Some pirate bacchanals last for weeks.

A DRUNKEN PIRATE AND HIS HEAD ARE SOON PARTED!

In their hunt for the notorious Blackbeard, **LIEUTENANT ROBERT MAYNARD** commanded the *Jane* with a 35-man crew, followed by midshipman Mr. Hyde on the *Ranger* with a crew of 25. Slowly and cautiously, the two sloops navigated their way through Ocracoke's winding channel, all the while being observed by Blackbeard aboard his *Adventure*. By nightfall on November 21, 1718, the two sloops had anchored and were preparing for an early morning attack. Unafraid, Blackbeard and his 18-man crew drank heavily throughout the night. The following day, Blackbeard lost the battle and, ultimately, his head.

Apparently, Blackbeard's demise by hangover was paid no heed by **BARTHOLOMEW "BLACK BART" ROBERTS**. On February 10, 1722, the British warship HMS *Swallow*, under Captain Challoner Ogle, caught up with Black Bart's 42-gun *Royal Fortune* off the coast of Cape Lopez. Roberts's crew was still feeling the effects of the previous night's celebration and were ill-prepared for battle. Roberts ordered his crew to man their stations and steered directly at the *Swallow* in an effort to blast his way into open seas. The ships exchanged a devastating broadside, and when the smoke cleared, Roberts was found slumped over one of his big guns, a blast of grapeshot to the throat.

PIRATES LOVE THEIR DRINK!

When pirates attacked a ship in the Gulf of Mexico headed to New Orleans, among the plundered booty was a hand-carved Italian marble fireplace mantel. Just as they were about to heave the mantel into the sea, one of the pirates read the attached shipping information and immediately stopped the action. The mantel was en route to Lynchburg, Tennessee, to the home of **MR. JACK DANIEL**. Because pirates have such an affinity for Jack Daniel's signature creation, Old No. 7 whiskey, they immediately repacked the mantel and shipped it to its rightful owner.

[FIG. II] OLD JACK DANIEL'S

WHAT'S FOR DINNER?

- **BARRELS OF FRESHWATER**, as many as the ship can hold. Depending on sailing location, replenishing sources may not be readily available.

- **FRESH FRUIT** prevents scurvy.

- **FRESH VEGETABLES** are eaten first, before they spoil.

- **FRESH MEAT AND SEAFOOD** seldom last more than a week unless cured/salted.

- **CHICKENS** for eggs; eaten when chicken feed runs out or if they die.

- **COWS** for milk; eaten when their food is gone or if they die.

- **HARDTACK BISCUITS** can last up to a year if kept dry, whereas bread lasts less than a week before becoming infested with weevils.

- **OIL, VINEGAR, AND VARIOUS SPICES.** Hot spices (chili peppers) are preferred because they mask the taste of spoiled/rancid food.

- **WINE, RUM, OR ANY OTHER SPIRIT.** Pirates will gladly drink *anything* with alcohol in it.

GROG

The word *grog* comes to us from "Old Grogram," the nickname given to British Rear Admiral Edward Vernon, who ordered his sailors' rum rations to be diluted, both to make them last and to prevent drunkenness. The diluting took place in a large barrel, commonly referred to as a *grog tub*.

1 ounce rum per every
7 to 9 ounces of water

1 or 2 teaspoons cane sugar

Lime juice

MIX WITHOUT ICE and serve straight up.

BUMBO / BUMBOO / BOMBO

A simple drink consisting of rum, water, sugar, and nutmeg, bumboo is far better tasting than grog.

2 ounces dark rum

1 ounce chilled water

2 brown/cane sugar cubes
or 2 teaspoons sugar syrup

Sprinkle of cinnamon

Sprinkle of nutmeg

COMBINE ALL INGREDIENTS, stir, and serve without ice.

RUMFUSTIAN

Rumfustian is a nasty stew-like mixture of sherry, gin, ale, egg yolks, and other ingredients, served hot and topped with a sprinkle of nutmeg. Interestingly enough, there is no rum in a rumfustian.

2 egg yolks

1 teaspoon sugar

2 ounces gin

2 ounces sherry

1 cup ale

Pinch ground cinnamon

Peel of 1 lemon

2 to 3 cloves

Pinch ground nutmeg

IN A BOWL, beat egg yolks with sugar. In a saucepan, combine gin, sherry, ale, cinnamon, lemon peel, and cloves and bring to the boiling point. Pour in egg/sugar mixture, stirring briskly. If any snot or blood happens to fall into the mixture, leave it. It'll definitely improve the taste! Serve in a mug and top with nutmeg.

HARDTACK BISCUITS

Hardtack biscuits are square crackers carried on ships as sustenance for long sea voyages because they are easy to make and last forever—even though with age they become hard as rocks!

4	cups flour
1½ to 2	cups water
3 to 4	teaspoons salt
2	tablespoons shortening (if available)

PREHEAT OVEN TO 400°F.

MIX INGREDIENTS in a bowl by hand, adding just enough water to make the mixture stick together. Dough should not stick to your hands. Roll dough and shape into a crude rectangle. Bake at 400°F for 1 hour. Remove from oven and cut dough into 3-by-3-inch squares. Using a fork or knife-tip, punch four rows of holes (four per row) into each square. Flip biscuits over and return to oven for 30 minutes. Cool.

SALMAGUNDI

Occasionally called "salmi," salmagundi—*salmagundis* is French for "hodgepodge"—is a cold salad-type dish featuring cooked meats, seafood, vegetables, fruit, leaves, nuts, and/or flowers, dressed with a mixture of oil, vinegar, and available spices. Some pirates prefer their salmagundi hot, more like a stew. The kind and amount of ingredients is up to you, but here is an example of how you might make this common dish:

CUT COLD ROAST CHICKEN, DUCK, AND ANY OTHER AVAILABLE MEAT into slices and place in a large pot. Add chopped onion and tarragon. Add olives, capers, raisins, mushrooms, almonds (and any other available nuts), peas, and red and white currants. Add lime, lemon, and orange slices/wedges. Cover with oil, vinegar, and lemon juice. Mix thoroughly. Serve cold, garnished with slices of orange and lemon.

BONE SOUP

Food shortages aboard pirate ships are common. When a lack of sustenance befalls the ship, desperate times require desperate measures. As long as we have fresh water to boil and there are fish/animal skeletons on board—the very reason we pirates save our bones—bone soup is in order. Granted, there ain't much to it, just a mealy broth with little (if any) taste and some beneficial nutrients but, compared to an empty bowl, plate, or mug, bone soup is akin to a lavish spread.

[FIG. 12] PIRATE GRUB

ROGUE STRATEGY

CURING/SALTING MEAT

Also known as salt-curing meat in brine.

1 Fill brine barrel halfway with hot water.

2 Add salt, using a ratio of 1 cup salt per 2 gallons water.

3 Add ½–1 cup vinegar and brown sugar (optional) to the mixture.

4 Cut meat into chunks and submerge in mixture.

5 Allow meat to soak for 6 to 7 days.

6 Remove meat from barrel, dry off, and place in sacks or in flour to keep flies and other insects away.

7 Hang in a cool, dry place (if available) to dry.

CURING/SALTING FISH

1 Remove head, scales, and guts. Toss in ocean as chum to attract sharks for more fun and games.

2 Bleed carcass thoroughly.

3 Rub with salt, completely covering fish and leaving no open spaces.

4 Pack fish into a large jar or barrel, skin side up, alternating a layer of fish with a layer of salt.

5 Seal jar/barrel and leave for 12 to 15 days.

6 Remove fish from barrel, rinse off salt, then place on flat surface and press fish as flat as possible to remove excess moisture.

7 If properly salted, fish flesh should be nearly translucent and no undo "rank" odor should exist.

8 Final drying should take place in a dry, well-ventilated area. Fish can be laid flat or, ideally, hung.

9 Final drying can take place in sunlight, although reserve this for the second day of the process, as immediate exposure to sunlight after removal from curing barrel may harden flesh or turn it yellow.

[FIG. 13] CURING MEAT

Of the said potatoes also they make a drink called Maiz.
They cut them into small slices, and cover them with hot
water. When they are well imbibed with water, they press them
through a coarse cloth, and the liquor that comes out, although
somewhat thick, they keep in vessel made for that purpose.
Here, after settling two or three days, it begins to work; and,
having thrown of its lees, is fit for drink. They use it with
great delight, and although the taste is somewhat sour, yet it is
very pleasant, substantial, and wholesome. The industry of this
composition is owing to the Indians, as well as many others,
which the ingenuity of those barbarians caused them to invent
both for the preservation and the pleasure of their own life.

ALEXANDRE EXQUEMELIN,
Bucaniers of America **(1684)**

CHARTED HOTSPOT

TORTUGA

This island off the coast of Haiti has long been a hideout for pirates; those who routinely hole up here like
to refer to themselves as the Brethren of the Coast.
It's a good place to stop for provisioning—the governor
once imported more than 1,600 prostitutes to "calm
things down"—so you might as well stay awhile and
enjoy yourself.

[FIG. 14] TORTUGA

scallywag!

CHAPTER
FIVE

DEAD RECKONING

*"I am bound to Madagascar,
with the design of making my own
fortune, and that of all the brave
fellows joined with me."*

—

HENRY EVERY

 Finders, keepers. Such is our mantra. Any prey we find is ours for the taking, assuming we're able to conquer it. And trust me, we don't have many problems in that arena. But the real key lies in the finding. There's a lot of sea to cover, and prizes tend not to announce their presence. So we have to look long and hard to earn our plunder. Thus, the success—and failure—of every pirate crew falls squarely on the shoulders of our seafaring, star-savvy captains.

Relying on a potent combination of common sense, seafaring experience, and good fortune, pirate captains usually set sail for a specific destination—either choosing a locale they know to be ripe with prizes, or plotting and anticipating a specific prize's course (such as through the Westward Passage or the Straits of Florida). Upon arrival in the general vicinity, the hunt begins.

Because of the oceans' immensity, blindly taking your chances in a huge and foreboding body of water is a foolish practice. Pirate captains prefer to concentrate on the smaller seas and waterways—areas that have been well documented and can be navigated quite easily via compass and highly annotated charts.

Accurate charts are a necessity for locating and maneuvering through back channels and shallow shoals, for planning ambushes, and for hiding or careening vessels. Therefore, it should come as no surprise that the best, most successful captains usually have the most detailed charts.

Pirate enemies aren't limited to heavily gunned warships. Many a vessel can become grounded on a sandbar, and ultimately be captured or destroyed, by a lack of local waterway knowledge. These problems befall even some of the most accomplished pirates. For example, Blackbeard's *Queen Anne's Revenge* met its demise on the sandbars off North Carolina's shores.

LATITUDE

This coordinate gives a location north or south of the equator.

KNOTS

In this case, *knots* refer to nautical miles per hour.
1 KNOT = 1.15077845 MILES PER HOUR
or **1.8519984 KILOMETERS PER HOUR**

LONGITUDE

The most commonly used coordinate to gauge east-west measurement.

WESTWARD PASSAGE

A strait between the easternmost side of Cuba and the northwest portion of Hispaniola (now Haiti), the Westward Passage connects the Atlantic Ocean to the Caribbean Sea. A major shipping lane, it's a favorite—and bountiful—hunting ground for prizes.

[FIG. 15] WESTWARD PASSAGE

A.

B.

C.

D.

[FIG. 16] NAVIGATIONAL TOOLS

NAVIGATION

ASTROLABE [FIG. 16A]
Dating back to 150 bce (Hipparchus is thought to be the inventor), astrolabes are used to locate and predict positions of stars and planets, allowing navigators to estimate their positions and even to tell time.

CROSS-STAFF [FIG. 16B]
A cross-staff—a.k.a. *Jacob's staff*—measures the altitude of the sun (day) or the North Star (night) to determine latitude.

BACKSTAFF [FIG. 16C]
A.k.a. *back-quadrant* or *Davis quadrant* (Captain John Davis invented a version of the backstaff in 1594), the backstaff is used to determine latitude. Similar to the cross-staff or astrolabe, instead of looking directly into the sun, you keep the sun to your back, hence the name. It provides the navigator with the sun's altitude by observing its shadow while simultaneously sighting the horizon. But perhaps its best feature is the fact that it prevents damage to the navigator's eyes.

OCTANT [FIG. 16D]
This measuring instrument came to fruition courtesy of Isaac Newton in 1699 when he invented the reflecting quadrant. Octant—a derivative of the Latin *octans*—means "eighth part of a circle"—and the octant's arc is ⅛ of a circle. It uses mirrors to reflect the path of light back to the observer, doubling the angle measured. Octants are similar to sextants but use only forty-five-degree angles.

NAVIGATION

SEXTANT [FIG. 16A]

Sextants measure the angle between any two visible objects, primarily a celestial object (star, sun) and the horizon. Taking the measurement—shooting the object, sighting the object, taking a sight—which consists of an angle and the time it was measured, allows a navigator to calculate his position on a nautical chart.

BRING 'EM NEAR/SPYGLASS [FIG. 16B]

Designed for the observation of remote objects, no ship should ever be without one. From sweeping the horizon for other ships' sails; identifying other ships' make, origin, or ordnance; verifying shore-based landmarks and batteries; or even scouting for shallow-water obstructions, bring 'em nears/spyglasses—a.k.a. captain's long-glasses—whether used from the bow or atop the main mast—can mean discovering a prize ripe for the plucking or, in the event the ship in your sights is a Royal Navy warship, saving your arse from dancing the hempen jig!

LODESTONE [FIG. 16C]

A naturally magnetic rock upon which pirates stroke a needle to magnetize it, thereby creating a handmade compass.

[FIG. 16] NAVIGATIONAL TOOLS

Once the sight of land is lost, the ability to calculate a ship's *latitude*—position north or south of the equator—requires observing the height of the sun by day and that of the North Star at night. Anything that obscures these reference points—clouds, fog, storm fronts, etc.—can play havoc with the readings, oftentimes causing ships to journey far off course.

To aid their endeavors, navigators use a variety of instruments, including the *astrolabe, cross-staff,* and *backstaff,* as well as the more sophisticated *octant* and *sextant.*

Pinpointing location also requires a longitude measurement. This is estimated by judging the ship's direction from a compass reading coupled with a fair amount of guesswork (a.k.a. *dead reckoning*) on the distance traveled by using a chip log and sandglass.

But of all our available tools, the time-honored compass has consistently proven to be the most vital navigational instrument aboard the ship. Since its magnetized needle always points north, we can, at a minimum, gauge our direction. A lost compass at sea is easily remedied if the ship carries a *lodestone.* Many captains are known to place their lodestones in decorative mountings to keep them safe, as well as to demonstrate their value.

Some think it remarkable that we pirates would even attempt, let alone successfully complete, sailing around the Cape of Good Hope or to the Spanish Main, considering our primitive tools and the overall inaccuracy of our charts, not to mention the vast areas of uncharted waters we have to cross during our voyages. Such is the lure of prizes and plunder. Men will gladly risk life and limb for booty.

INSULÆ AMERICANÆ in Oceano Septentrionali ac REGIONES ADIACENTES, a C. de May usque ad Lineam Æquinoctialem. Per Nicolaum Visscher. Cum Privilegio Ordinum Hollandiæ et Westfrisiæ.

Hunting Grounds
& Strongholds
of the West Indies

CIRCA 1686

The 20th Day of May, our bark being about 3 leagues a head of our ship, sailed over a rocky shoal, on which there was but 4 fathom water and abundance of fish swimming about the rocks. They imagin'd by this that the land was not far off; so they clapt on a wind with the bark's head to the north, and being past the shoal lay by for us. When we came up with them, **Captain Teat** came aboard us, and related what he had seen. We were then in Lat. 12 d. 55 m. steering West. The island Guam is laid down in Lat. 13 d. N. by the Spaniards, who are masters of it, keeping it as a baiting place as they go to the Philippine islands.

It was well for **Captain Swan** that we got sight of it before our provision was spent, of which we had but enough for 3 more days; for as I was afterwards informed, the men had contrived first to kill **Captain Swan** and eat him when the victuals was gone, and after him all of us who were accessory in promoting the undertaking this voyage. This made **Captain Swan** say to me after our arrival at Guam, "Ah! ~~Dampier~~, you would have made them a poor meal." For I was as lean as the captain was lusty and fleshy.

WILLIAM DAMPIER,
A New Voyage Around the World (**1697**)

ROGUE STRATEGY

How to Make a Compass

1 Take a sewing needle from your one-legged sailmaker and repeatedly stroke it in the same direction with a magnet. (If you don't have a magnet, use silk.)

2 Suspend the needle from a piece of thread, attached to the needle's center.

3 Make sure the needle remains suspended parallel to the deck and it will slowly rotate, ultimately pointing north.

[FIG. 17] PIRATE COMPASS

THOSE WHO PLUNDER AND RUN AWAY LIVE TO PLUNDER ANOTHER DAY.

Following the plundering of the *Ganj-i-Sawai* in the Indian Ocean, **HENRY EVERY** sailed his *Fancy* to the island of New Providence, where he divided the booty among his crew and disappeared to parts unknown. Many of Every's crewmen, however, did not follow their captain's lead. They remained on the island and, courtesy of their exotic spending sprees, were caught and executed for crimes of piracy.

HE WHO GIVES THE BEST GIFTS LIVES.

In 1861, during an eighteen-month plundering escapade, **BARTHOLOMEW SHARP** captured the Spanish ship *El Santo Rosario*. Among the booty was, in his own words, "a great Book full of Sea-Charts and Maps, containing a very accurate and exact description of all the Ports, Soundings, Creeks, Rivers, Capes, and Coasts belonging to the South Sea, and all the Navigations usually performed by the Spaniards in that Ocean." This priceless atlas of Spanish sailing secrets—illustrating coastlines from California to Cape Horn—was presented to King Charles II and helped to acquit Sharp from the charge of piracy, for which he would have been hanged.

I MAY BE GONE, BUT MY PIRATE SOUL IS ETERNAL!

Buccaneer and nautical explorer **WILLIAM DAMPIER** kept detailed journals of his exploits attacking Portobello with **CAPTAIN BARTHOLOMEW SHARP** in 1679, and raiding the East Indies in 1683 with **CAPTAIN CHARLES SWAN**. The published journals quickly became a popular four-volume set. Dampier's accounts of the South Seas were so valuable that **CAPTAIN WOODES ROGERS** engaged him as a pilot for his around-the-world privateering expedition of 1708–1711.

ALEXANDER EXQUEMELIN was another notable piratical author who joined the buccaneers as a surgeon in 1666. His remarkable book—*Bucaniers of America*—published in 1684, contains numerous exciting and bloody pirate stories. Among them: Henry Morgan's raids on the Spanish Main, Francois L'Olonnais's sacking of Maracaibo and cutting victims to pieces, and Roche Brasiliano's brutal torturing of Spaniards by roasting them alive on wooden spits. Exquemelin's work is recognized as the ultimate reference on the lives and adventures of the great buccaneers.

How to Chart a Course

Successful navigation can be achieved quite easily by plotting a course on a nautical chart. For every leg of the course, figure distance, speed, time, and the heading to be traveled.

1. Using a parallel ruler—or better yet, a parallel plotter, designed to roll without sliding—draw a straight line from your point of departure to your intended destination, or from your departure point to the first turn on your course.

2. Draw as many lines as needed to plot the entire trip.

3. Lay parallel ruler/parallel plotter along the drawn line.

4. Roll plotter to the nearest compass rose on the chart until the edge intersects the crossed lines at the center.

5. Where the course line intersects the inside degree circle is the magnetic bearing. Mark this course above the plotted line (in degrees magnetic).

6. Repeat for every line in the plotted course.

7. Figure distance for each individual course in nautical miles using the dividers and the chart's distance scale (usually found at the top or bottom).

8. Calculate the time it will take to travel each course by determining speed (knots), based on intended cruising speed and current conditions. Write this atop the course line, next to the bearing.

9. Continue calculating the time required to run each course by multiplying the distance of the course times sixty.

10. Divide result by the predetermined/estimated speed (knots).

11. Final result is the amount of time (minutes/seconds) to complete plotted course.

12. Repeat this process for every course and write the result on the course line.

13. When you begin your journey, make sure to use a sandglass for every leg of the trip and record the time spent on each leg.

14. Be sure the vessel is at proper plotted speed and that your direction is correct. Even a minor variance will throw off your bearings.

15. Be sure to reset sandglass for each new course (new line) on the chart. Failure to do so will throw you off course—and you should be thrown overboard.

How to Navigate by the Stars

Celestial navigation is the oldest means of reckoning. To aid in this endeavor, there are a few major constellations that every would-be navigator must know.

- -

1 For the Northern Hemisphere, use the Big Dipper and Cassiopeia. Both are visible year-round, revolving around the North Star (Polaris).

2 The Big Dipper looks somewhat like a frying pan—long handle, rectangular pan. If you're looking at the "pan," draw an imaginary straight line from the two farthest stars, extending perpendicular to the Dipper's tail. This line will point directly to Polaris.

3 Cassiopeia is on the other side of Polaris, opposite Big Dipper. It resembles a W, turned on its side.

4 Polaris makes an arrow with one of Cassiopeia's points and is nearly equidistant between the two.

5 Polaris doesn't move (in appearance); other stars rotate around it.

6 Measure the angle between the horizon and Polaris to determine your latitude. Polaris is on the horizon at the equator (0 degrees), directly above the North Pole (90 degrees).

7 The angle between the horizon and Polaris is your current latitude.

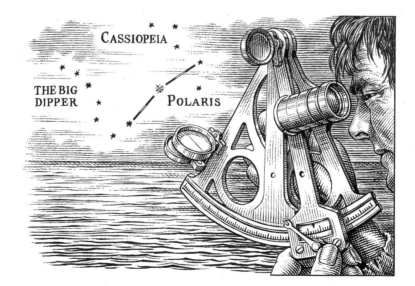

CASSIOPEIA

THE BIG
DIPPER

POLARIS

[FIG. 18] CELESTIAL NAVIGATION

no quarter!

CHAPTER
SIX

PREPARE TO BOARD

"No time wasted, straight up alongside, every gun brought to play, and the prize boarded."

———

CALICO JACK RACKAM

(ON CAPTURING SHIPS . . . AND WOMEN)

*P*irates don't work for wages. We live by the simple motto, "No prey, no pay." Unlike privateers—who only attack vessels from nations their king, queen, or country is at odds with—pirates have no such limitations. Any vessels we see are fair game. And once prey is sighted, all it takes is a majority vote from the crew and the hunt begins! Iron and lead first, followed by steel, this is the piratical way, the modus operandi by which we carry out our sinister trade. If the prey ship doesn't surrender, first comes a massive cannonball onslaught from the big guns. Next comes the "softening" of the prey via precision musket marksmanship and ungodly gunfire from the swivel guns (packed with grapeshot), blunderbusses (firing scattershot), and close-aim pistol fire. Finally, the call to board is given and a maniacal horde of pirates will crest the gunwales and swarm the prey's deck, swinging boarding axes, slashing with cutlasses, and firing flintlocks.

In the initial stages of the stalk, a pirate ship will shadow its prey while the captain determines whether the odds of victory (based on the opposing ship's armament and number of visible crewmen) are in their favor, exactly as advocated by famed Chinese military general and strategist, Sun Tzu, some 2,200 years ago. Assuming the captain likes what he sees, the pirate ship will move in close, hoist the *Jolly Roger* so the other crew knows exactly who—and what—they are dealing with, and then fire a warning shot across the prize's bow, giving them an opportunity to surrender with little or no bloodshed. But the perfunctory "surrender or else" cannon shot isn't the only frightening tactic employed to signify that a floating spectacle of death is in their midst. The pirate crew will also begin *vaporing*—screaming vicious war cries and horrific death threats while flailing and banging cutlasses and boarding axes against the gunwales of the ship. And if a musician is aboard, his furious fiddle play, blaring horn blasts, or ominous drumbeats will add to the raucous din, ratcheting up the crew's unbearable chanting to what sounds like a fever pitch straight from the depths of hell.

[FIG. 19] PIRATE CREW READY TO BOARD

LOAD AND FIRE A CANNON

1. A pirate ship's great guns (cannons) are mounted atop four-wheeled carriages, allowing them to roll in and out of the gun ports for faster firing and reloading.

2. Prior to loading, it is absolutely vital that a member of the gun crew inspect the barrel to insure it is empty and clean. It is equally vital that the cannon inspector *not* be smoking a pipe while performing the task for obvious reasons. If he is, rest assured it will be the last time he makes that mistake—or any mistake for that matter!

3. If the cannon has recently been fired, the bore must first be swabbed with a damp sponge to remove any remaining live embers before reloading, otherwise there will be no live gun crew!

4. To load the cannon, a four-man gun crew has to run the gun inside the ship's gunwale and put a powder bag (charge) down the front of the barrel, followed by the cannonball.

5. A ramrod is then used to push the ball and charge together at the bottom of the barrel.

6. Each cannon has a vent hole drilled at the top rear of the barrel, allowing a fuse to be inserted, conveying flame to the charge. Most fuses are approximately six inches long, giving gun crews approximately ten seconds to get clear and cover their ears before the cannon discharges.

7. As soon as the cannon is loaded, the gun is run out through the gunport and the gunner sets the aim.

8. Once the command to fire is given, the fuse is lit and *BOOM!*

9. Although a typical four-pounder can fire a *roundshot* (cannonball) about a thousand yards, maximum accuracy is only about five hundred feet, so all shots must be properly positioned.

10. The loading and firing routine is repeated over and over and over again until the prey surrenders or the gun crew runs out of ammunition.

[FIG. 20] FIRING A CANNON

If all goes well, this barrage of sound and barbarism will cause the prey vessel to strike her colors, signifying her submission. However, while we prefer to capture a prize without a fight—avoiding the many gruesome injuries that go hand in hand with battles at sea, not to mention the very real possibility of having our ship damaged to the point of sinking, thereby scattering our hard-earned plunder across the ocean floor—we are ready, willing, and most certainly able to attack and slaughter anything and everything in our path.

If the prey refuses to strike her colors, we often hoist a red flag, declaring *no quarter*. Immediately, our pirate vessel will unleash her great guns, intent on destroying the prize ship's mast—to prevent her from escaping— as well as to cause as much topside damage as possible, for sinking the ship would be a foolish undertaking; the prize is far more valuable afloat than in Neptune's garden, to be used as another pirate ship or sold/traded later on.

When in small-arms range, the harassment will intensify via strategic musket fire, targeting the navigator and gun crews to prevent evasive maneuvers or return cannon fire. Boarders—armed with a wicked array of loaded flintlocks and freshly sharpened cutlasses or boarding axes, stand- ing ready along the rail as our pirate vessel navigates amidships—throw *grenadoes* and *caltrops* onto the prize's deck, adding to the calamity and confusion. When the distance between ships is no more, grappling hooks are tossed fore and aft, lashing the two vessels together. To prevent sepa- ration, the ends of the irons are customarily attached to long lengths of chain to prevent them from being severed by prey ship crewmen. The final action before the actual boarding involves skilled marksmen making surgi- cally precise shots, clearing not only the deck but also the masts and spars aloft in a concerted effort to protect the boarding party.

The call to board will immediately follow, coming from the quartermas- ter upon the captain's signal. The best attack plan for boarding a vessel requires the pirate ship to lay alongside her prize, ideally from the weather

GIVE NO QUARTER, TAKE NO QUARTER.

Beginning with the early privateering days of **SIR FRANCIS DRAKE** (a.k.a. "The Dragon"), when the red flag is hoisted it means *no quarter* to the prey. No mercy. No survivors. This simple act usually knocks the fight out of all but the most pigheaded captains, the majority of whom pay for their stubbornness with their lives and, sadly, the lives of their crew.

LOOKS CAN BE DECEIVING.

In January 1698, **WILLIAM KIDD**, then privateer captain of the *Adventure Galley*, and later a pirate, spotted a ship in the distance flying French colors. Kidd quickly replaced his English flag (Union Jack) with a French flag and then sailed close enough to the large *Quedah Merchant* to fire a shot across her bow and order her surrender. The captain showed Kidd a French pass, hoping this would grant him freedom to sail. With a sly smile, Kidd ordered his ship's French flag be hauled to the deck and hoisted the Union Jack once again, thus declaring the *Quedah Merchant* a legal prize.

JOLLY ROGER

A Jolly Roger is a flag that identifies the ship flying it as a pirate vessel. While the skull and crossbones is the most common of these flags, many great pirate captains have custom colors that further identify exactly who is attacking. As such, some Jolly Rogers elicit significantly more fear than others. **CALICO JACK RACKAM**'s design is a skull with a pair of crossed swords below it. **BLACKBEARD**'s flag pictures a devil stabbing a bleeding heart with a spear. **CHRISTOPHER CONDENT**'s flag features not one but three skulls and crossbones. And **EDWARD LOW**'s flag shows an eerie red skeleton against a black background.

[FIG. 21] JOLLY ROGER

BOARDING WITH EVIL INTENT

GRENADOES

Pirates use two types of grenadoes (a.k.a. grenades): those designed to obscure and confuse, and those intended to maim and kill.

Smoke grenades—ceramic shells stuffed with tar and rags with a fuse protruding from the top—are lit and thrown onto a prize's deck, where they smash open and create dense black smoke-screens.

The other grenades (a specialty of Blackbeard's) are empty bottles packed with black powder, shot, and small pieces of lead. The explosion on or below deck will do little, if any, damage to the prize but will produce brutal, often fatal, injuries among the prey ship's crew.

CALTROPS
("CROWSFEET")

Made of scrap iron and featuring (at least) four wickedly sharp points, caltrops are designed to be tossed onto the deck of a ship and, no matter how they land, always have one point facing up, thereby delivering painful piercing injuries to barefoot and fallen sailors.

BOARDING PIKE

A long wooden shaft measuring ten to twenty feet in length with a sharpened steel or iron spearhead affixed to the end.

[FIG. 22] BATTLE ON DECK

gauge (between wind and prey) and amidships. A clever pirate captain will maneuver his ship between the wind and his prey, putting the bow alongside his enemy's waist, so that his midship is snugged up close to the prey's quarter, allowing the pirate crew to board fast and aggressively by her shrouds.

Trust me, if the prize's crew was terrified when they first saw the Jolly Roger, the sight of a murderous horde climbing over their gunwales, weapons up and ready, intent on delivering agony and death with every trigger stroke or swing causes many to jump ship, hoping the sea will be less savage than the invaders.

Oftentimes, it is.

Boarding is far from serene and systematic. With plunder on our minds and murder in our hearts, we'll use any means necessary to get onto the prize. For some, it's as simple as using boarding pikes to create a little distance between themselves and the prey's crew. Others, hoping for a sneak attack of sorts, will swing from the riggings and drop down on the unsuspecting crewmen. And then there are those who simply leap over the gunwales, hacking, slashing, and shooting their way into the violent fray.

The battle on deck is a brutal and bloody business. There are no rules. Bashing in an opponent's skull with a boarding ax, or slicing off limbs and digits, are all common practices. The goal is to win at all costs. Fight fast and fight furious. And don't get caught up with one opponent or opponents for too long lest you fall victim to an attack from behind. Once pirates engage in battle, there are only two outcomes: victory (and the spoils that come with it) or death, either on the ship or via execution for piracy later on.

Once the enemy crew is vanquished—either by total annihilation or, if they are smart, surrender—anything of use or value is plundered. Coins, jewels, precious metals, medicine, food and water, weapons—if it can be sold, spent, or used, we take it.

CUTLASS [FIG. 23A]

Shorter but thicker in width than a standard cavalry saber, the majority of cutlasses—particularly those of the eighteenth-century French Navy—are slightly curved and are the preferred sidearm for every country's navy. You can swing them with reckless abandon without fear of getting caught in the riggings. Most cutlasses have a *fuller* (sometimes referred to as a *blood groove*) running from the hilt to within seven inches of the point. Pirates are famous for using cutlasses, but there is no evidence to support the widespread belief that Caribbean buccaneers invented them.

DUSAGGE CUTLASS [FIG. 23B]

While all cutlasses can inflict nasty wounds, the German-made *Dusagge* cutlass is especially fearsome, thanks to the many serrations on both sides of its broad, curved blade. However, the serrations weren't added for greater effectiveness against flesh and bone—they are intended to catch and slash through rigging lines commonly encountered during shipboard combat.

BELAYING PIN [FIG. 23C]

A solid hardwood bar (one to three feet long) inserted along the inside of a ship's bulwarks to secure lines. Because of its bulbous top portion and cylindrical shaft, a belaying pin makes a formidable club/impact weapon.

MARLINSPIKE [FIG. 23D]

Made of iron or steel with a pointed end, marlinspikes (ranging from six to eighteen inches long) are used for a variety of deck chores, from separating strands of rope to prying open crates and barrels. Small and concealable, they are also the perfect size to be used as dagger-like weapons, making them ideal for those with mutiny on their mind.

GRAPESHOT [FIG. 23E]

Loosely packed metal slugs loaded in a canvas bag or packed directly into the swivel guns. This type of load is often improvised in the form of rocks, shards of glass, chain links, and any other metal scraps lying around.

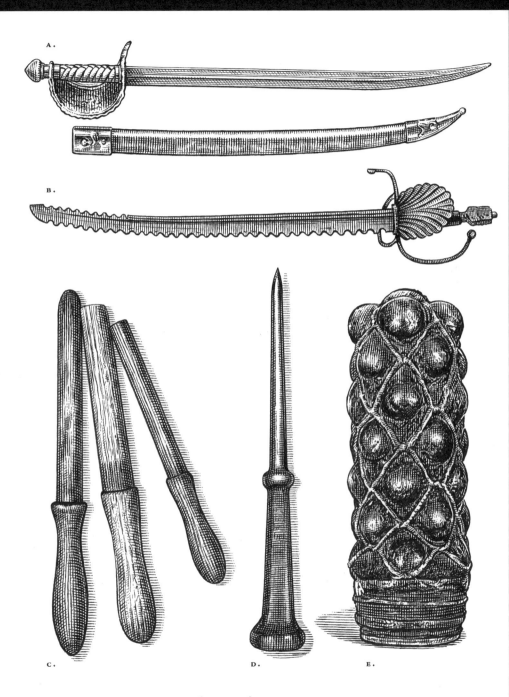

[FIG. 23] WEAPONS

How to Use a Cutlass

While many pirates simply prefer to swing and hack like maniacs with no real method to their madness, others take a far more artful approach.

- Striking major organs (heart, lungs, brain, etc.) in the torso and head will end a fight quickly; however, there are less defensible areas you can attack to curtail a battle just as fast.

- Feint for the head/torso, then strike at the extremities. Slicing off an opponent's elbow, especially while his sword is raised or "cocked and locked," will disarm him, literally.

- Or feint high and go low, slicing out your enemy's legs from under him. This maneuver is extremely hard to block, and, even if your opponent is still among the living, the battle is over—he won't be able to come after you.

- Never jump in the air to attack. This commits you. When gravity takes over, you're coming down whether you like it or not. A skilled opponent can simply step back, out of harm's way, and mount an offensive when you land.

- The same holds true for spinning. Even if you're extremely fast, turning your back on an opponent, especially one armed with an edged weapon, is very risky and usually has disastrous results.

- The only time you should risk clashing swords with an opponent is to deflect his blade from your body. The risk of breaking your weapon is too great. Better to wait for an opening and then strike.

- Control your attack. Don't overswing. A big miss, in which your momentum carries your blade past your intended target, will leave you defenseless, exposed, and ripe for the picking.

- Use a secondary weapon in tandem with the cutlass. While some pirates are demons with both a dagger and cutlass, other weapons, such as nets, rope coils, and lengths of chain can confuse, distract, or even trap an opponent, making delivering the coup de grâce with your cutlass that much easier.

- And yes, it's far easier to forego your cutlass and simply shoot your opponent with a flintlock.

PIRATE MENTOR

You don't need balls to have balls!

Anchored off the north coast of Jamaica in October 1720, **CALICO JACK** and his male crewmen were getting raucously drunk below decks when they were surprised by a heavily armed privateer sloop hunting down pirates. Calico Jack's drunken crew hid in the hold but **ANNE BONNY** and **MARY READ** immediately sprang into action with pistols firing, curses flying, and cutlasses and axes slashing and hacking at everyone in their path. When they realized the battle was lost, Mary turned her rage below decks and fired a shot down into the ship's hold, screaming for the crew to "come up and fight like men."

[FIG. 24] ANNE BONNY & MARY READ

Prisoners, for the most part, are treated fairly. Despite many tales to the contrary, women and children are almost never harassed (or worse). Sailors, depending on their desire and skills, are sometimes given the opportunity to join our pirate crew and many jump at the chance. Those who opt out of the brethren are usually cast off in a long boat (with some provisions, for not all pirates are complete bastards) or left on the first island or landmass we encounter. But the enemy captain often faces an entirely different fate—a fate decided by his own crew.

Many pirate captains take it upon themselves to mete out a little maritime justice. They ask the conquered prey ship's crew whether their captain was an honorable and just man, worthy of a continued existence. If the defeated crew supports their leader, the captain is spared. But, if it turned out the captain is brazen, cruel, or a poor shepherd of the sea, Davy Jones is delivered another tortured soul, one with a title before his name.

When it's over, we return to the pirate ship, attend to our injured, divvy up the booty—every man gets a share; those suffering severe but survivable wounds get extra—and set off in search of another prize.

The Barbadoes ships kept an easy sail till the Pyrates came up with them, and then **Bartholomew Roberts** gave them a gun, expecting they would have immediately struck to his piratical flag, but instead thereof, he was forced to receive the fire of a broadside, with three huzzas at the same time. So that an engagement ensued, but **Roberts** being hardly put to it, was obliged to crowd all the sail the sloop would bear, to get off. The galley failing pretty well, kept company for a long while, keeping a constant fire, which gall'd the Pyrate. However, at length by throwing over their guns, and other heavy goods, and thereby light'ning the vessel, they, with much ado, got clear. But **Roberts** could never endure a Barbadoes man afterwards, and when any ships belonging to that island fell in his way, he was more particularly severe to them than others.

CAPTAIN CHARLES JOHNSON,
A General History of the Pyrates (1726)

JUST BECAUSE I'M CORNERED DOESN'T MEAN I'M DEFEATED.

In 1669, after **HENRY MORGAN** sacked *Maracaibo*, his ships were trapped inside the bottle-shaped Lake Maracaibo by three heavily armed Spanish ships—the 40-gun *Magdalena*, the 30-gun *San Luis*, and the 30-gun *Soledad*—all waiting at the narrow mouth of the lake for Morgan to exit. So Morgan directed his buccaneers to convert one of his captured ships into a "fire ship." First, they filled the vessel with black powder, pitch, tar, and sulfur. Then they positioned drums in the gun ports to give the appearance of cannons, along with vertical timbers disguised as crewmembers manning weapons. Finally, they cut the ship's planks to effect a devastating, shattering force when the gunpowder exploded. Captain Morgan then sailed his pirate flotilla into the mouth of the lake with the fire ship leading the way, steering directly toward the *Magdalena*. The fire ship crashed into the monstrous 40-gunner and exploded, obliterating the vessel. Morgan's force then captured the *Soledad*. In an interesting twist, the Spanish elected to sink the *San Luis* themselves to prevent it from becoming yet another Morgan prize.

MY SWORD IS BIGGER THAN YOUR SWORD!

In the seventeenth century, **FRANÇOIS L'OLONNAIS**, the "cutlass buccaneer," was extremely proficient with a cutlass, both as a weapon and as an interrogation tool. When it came to getting his captives to talk, François would hit the unlucky individuals with the flat of his cutlass's blade until they divulged where they'd hidden their valuables.

Dagger

Daggers are every pirate's general-purpose knife and last-ditch backup weapon. Smaller blades, no longer than six inches, are both easier to conceal and easier to wield, especially in close-quarters combat.

[FIG. 25] DAGGER

How to Sharpen a Knife/Dagger

Common mistakes when it comes to sharpening any blade include a failure
to establish a new edge, uncontrolled bevel angles, and leaving the final bevel too rough.

1. First, pick an angle at which to sharpen your knife. If you already know what angle your knife is sharpened at, stay with it. Otherwise, choose an angle of 10 to 30 degrees per side.

2. The shallower the angle, the sharper the edge; steeper angles are far more durable.

3. Select the angle/edge based on use. If it's defensive only, sharpness is key. If it's primarily for camp use, go with a more durable grind.

4. When in doubt, 17 degrees is a good compromise.

5. Use an angle guide (if available) to control your edge's angle. Without an angle guide, you'll have to do it by hand, which is difficult and requires a solid perception of angles.

6. For a symmetrical edge, drag the knife across a lubricated (oil or water) stone in the *opposite* direction you would move it to slice a thin layer off the stone. This will allow a *burr* to form, prolonging the sharpening stone's life.

7. Continue grinding at this angle until the grind goes approximately halfway through the steel.

8. Now flip the knife over and sharpen the other side of the blade until a new edge is created. This will be easy to determine when a burr has been raised (one bevel is ground until it meets another). Although not always visible, you should be able to feel it with your finger.

9. Flip the knife and sharpen the opposite side of the blade. For a single-sided grind/chisel grind, do not flip.

10. Remove the burr by holding the blade at the same angle and moving it in the opposite direction as in the previous steps.

11. If you plan on using your knife for *push cutting* (cutting straight down without sliding blade across the object, used more with camp knives than combat/defensive knives), you may elect to polish or *strop* the edge—sharpen/realign the edge without removing any metal, usually with a flexible strip of leather or canvas.

12. A good indicator of a sharp edge without dull spots is its ability (or rather its inability) to reflect light. Dull blades will reflect light along the edge; sharp blades will not.

13. Never test your blade's sharpness by dragging a finger along the edge. Instead, try cutting a loosely held piece of paper, or slice someone else's finger or neck.

How to Throw
a Dagger

---

1 Determine the dagger's *fulcrum* (center of gravity) by balancing it sideways across your index finger, adjusting its position until level.

2 With the blade facing you, grip the dagger with your thumb and the side of your index finger on the fulcrum. Your thumb (top) and finger (bottom) should cross at a 90-degree angle; the dagger is technically still balanced on the side of your finger, thumb holding it in place.

3 Raise your elbow to eye level (thumb facing sky), bending your arm so the dagger is a few inches above and to the side of your head.

4 Step forward with your opposite leg and bring your arm down and out in one smooth motion.

5 Wrist should be straight but relaxed.

6 As your arm becomes fully extended, look down your wrist, lining up your thumb with the handle of the dagger and the intended target.

7 Once your hand reaches eye level, draw an imaginary line from the tip of your thumb, up the handle's center, and through the target (at butt of handle). This is the throw's release point.

8 Release with your thumb first, allowing the dagger to roll off your index finger. This will initiate the rotation, stabilizing the dagger.

9 Timing is everything. Too much pressure and the dagger will over-rotate, flying at a down angle, thereby missing low.

10 Throwing your dagger should only be considered under "worst-case scenario" circumstances. Unless you hit and incapacitate your enemy, throwing your only weapon away will leave you unarmed and at a severe disadvantage over an armed opponent, and then you can kiss your arse good-bye.

How to Defend
Against a Dagger

To defend against a **THRUST**, whereby your attacker stabs straight in toward your gut, the dagger in his right hand:

1 First and foremost, always give your attacker less body (and vital areas) to target by turning sideways, similar to a boxer's stance, your weight balanced. This holds true for any form of defense.

2 Hop, step, or slide backward, pulling your stomach as far away as possible from the dagger thrust.

3 Simultaneously, hunch over and shoot both hands (with thumbs overlapped) on top of the dagger hand's wrist and extend your elbows, exerting downward force.

4 Tightly grasp your attacker's wrist and redirect dagger—using attacker's momentum—past your right side and up into the air with a pulling action that maintains the attacker's arm in an extended (and now vulnerable) posture.

5 Step under attacker's arm with your left leg (your back to attacker).

6 Quickly and violently yank the attacker's arm (elbow) down forcibly on top of your left shoulder, snapping your opponent's arm in half. If you hear a sickening *crack* and a scream, you did it right!

[FIG. 26] DAGGER DEFENSE

To defend against an **OUTSIDE-IN SLASH**, whereby your attacker slashes right to left—as if aiming for your face—the dagger in his right hand:

1. Sidestep right while pulling your head away from the direction of the dagger and simultaneously blocking the attack with your left hand on the inside of the attacker's dagger hand (in this case, right) at the wrist.

2. Tightly grasp the wrist with your left hand and hold away from your face.

3. Using your right hand, shoot a ridge hand (the web of skin between thumb and forefinger) blow into the attacker's throat.

4. Bring right hand onto the attacker's wrist to support your left-handed grasp.

5. Step through with your right leg (your back to attacker) under the attacker's arm and swing dagger hand into a high arc as you continue to step through with your left leg.

6. Continue the momentum of the arc by finishing with a final thrust of the dagger hand into the attacker's own gut.

7. Step back and watch as the dagger-impaled attacker slumps to the floor.

- -

To defend against an **INSIDE-OUT SLASH**, whereby your attacker makes a backhanded slash at your face (usually following a missed outside-in slash), the dagger in his right hand:

1. Sidestep left while pulling your head away from the direction of the dagger and simultaneously blocking the attack with your right hand on the back of the attacker's dagger hand at the wrist.

2. Tightly grasp the attacker's wrist and hold away from your face.

3. Twist your hips to the right, throwing your left forearm into the back of the attacker's elbow, as your right hand pulls his wrist.

4. This maneuver will turn your forearm into a fulcrum. The attacker's shoulder and wrist are moving in an opposite direction of his elbow, causing it to dislocate and making him drop the dagger.

5. Finish off your now-injured would-be attacker in any number of ways, or simply pick up the dagger and walk away.

6. The heck with just walking away. You're a pirate. Kill your enemy with his own weapon!

aye!

CHAPTER
SEVEN

STEAL
THIS SHIP

"Every normal man must be tempted
at times to spit on his hands,
hoist the black flag, and begin slitting throats."
—

HENRY LEWIS MENCHEN

From the nimble, shallow-draft *sloops* to the robust, multi-mast *frigates*, and vessels of every possible size and description in between, pirates have myriad ships from which to choose. But regardless of which vessel is selected as a mobile base of operations, it must fulfill three important criteria.

First, the ship must be a suitable means of housing. Pirates live where they work, so the ship needs to be large enough to properly contain and support the entire crew, along with all the life-sustaining provisions, necessary tools and weaponry, and, perhaps most important, the hard-earned plunder.

Second, as a means of transportation, the ship has to be both swift and strong with no exceptions. Swift in that she is fast and nimble enough to outsail and outmaneuver her prey, while simultaneously being able to escape from her enemies (of which there are many). Strong in that she can handle whatever Mother Nature throws at her, with conditions varying greatly depending on the body of water she roams.

Finally, the ship needs to be sufficiently armed to the point that, upon first sight, she is instantly viewed as a force of fear and destruction, persuasive enough to compel many (if not all) of her prey to abandon all hope and surrender immediately or suffer the consequences. By the same token, for those marks who do not submit, or for any enemies who see fit to attack her, the ship's bite has to equal or exceed its bark.

Once the vessel of choice is procured by whatever means possible—preferably via plunder or theft, for no true pirate would ever stoop so low as to actually *buy* a ship—the ship is refitted to suit the pirates' specific needs.

In most cases, the first order of business is to eliminate much of the interior space normally divided into individual compartments for carrying cargo. The crew will remove the bulkheads, knock down cabin walls, cut down quarterdecks, and make the ship flush fore and aft. Large holes are

Never pay your crew; reward them with shares of the booty!

In 1692, **THOMAS TEW**, with a commission from the Governor of Bermuda in his pocket, set sail as directed to attack French holdings on Africa's Gambia River. However, once at sea, Tew assembled his crew on deck and explained that not only was there little to gain in Africa, there would be great danger in gaining it! Tew then suggested a far more lucrative bounty: the Great Mogul of India's treasure-laden ships in the Red Sea. He was immediately greeted by resounding cheers, along with an all-hands cry of "A gold chain or a wooden leg, we'll stand by you!" And with that historic decree, the privateer was transformed into the *Rhode Island Pirate*.

Never buy a ship when you can simply steal one!

In 1694, **HENRY EVERY**, a former midshipman with the British Royal Navy, was serving as first mate aboard the *Charles II* when he led a successful "soft mutiny"—rumor has it **CAPTAIN CHARLES GIBSON**, a notorious drunk, was ashore in a rum-induced slumber—and slipped out of the Spanish port of La Coruna with the vessel and its crew. Every renamed the 46-gun frigate *Fancy*, hoisted new colors, and set sail for the Indian Ocean, where he boarded and plundered every vessel in sight for the next two years, spreading his villainous reputation across the sea.

In 1724, the soon-to-be notorious **JOHN GOW** used more aggressive methods to commandeer a vessel and jump-start his piracy career. He was a second mate aboard the trading vessel *Caroline*; and the shipboard atmosphere was one of serious discontent. **CAPTAIN OLIVER FERNEAU**, by all accounts a mean-spirited cur, overheard talk of a mutiny and had his officers prepare a cache of firearms to put down the uprising. The only problem: John Gow, one of those trusted officers, was the leader of the revolt. It was Gow himself who dispatched Captain Ferneau via flintlock and threw his body overboard. Renaming the ship *Revenge*, Gow gained infamy pillaging and plundering ships in the seas surrounding France, Portugal, and Spain.

TOOLS OF THE TRADE

THE SHIPS

SLOOP

Fast and agile with a shallow draft, sloops are commonly rigged with a single large mainsail but can feature additional sails that are lateen- or square-rigged. Although sloops can be as large as a hundred tons, they are usually smaller.

SCHOONER

Narrow-hulled, shallow-drafted, and with two masts, these vessels usually weigh in at less than a hundred tons. Extremely fast, capable of waiting in shallow coves to surprise unsuspecting prey, and yet still large enough to carry an ample crew, the schooner is one of our favorite vessels.

BRIGANTINE

A small double-mast ship outfitted with both sails and oars, brigantines are a favorite of our brethren operating in the Mediterranean Sea.

[FIG. 27A] SLOOP

[FIG. 27B] SCHOONER

[FIG. 27C] BRIGANTINE

FRIGATE

One step down from a ship-of-the-line, these triple-mast warships feature a raised quarterdeck and forecastle, and usually have somewhere between twenty-four to forty guns. Very few pirate captains command frigates, mainly because most pirates prefer to flee from these formidable vessels and, as such, only a handful are ever captured and converted for piratical usage.

[FIG. 27D] FRIGATE

SHIP-OF-THE-LINE

Also referred to as a *man-o'-war*, these vessels are true battleships. They have three masts, weigh in around a thousand tons, and average in the vicinity of seventy guns, with some carrying more than a hundred. Only three sea-power nations—England, France, and Spain—have these behemoths in their fleets. Unless you have a death wish, they should be avoided at all costs.

[FIG. 27E] SHIP-OF-THE-LINE

also carved into the ship's sides to create new gun ports, assuming sufficient ports don't already exist. *Swivel guns* are mounted in stanchions along the gunwales. Anything else decreasing the speed and handling of the ship is tossed overboard. Pirate ships have crews that significantly outnumber those on traditional merchant ships, and the men need room to roam and carry out attacks. Pirates are fond of outnumbering and overwhelming victims—the en masse, "screaming avalanche" approach works very well—so space is always of the essence.

Although most pirates prefer smaller and faster sloops like schooners and brigantine ships (which are also easier to steal), there are some advantages to the larger triple-mast, square-rigged warships used by the likes of Captain Kidd (34-gun *Adventure Galley*), William Moody (35-gun *Rising Sun*), Blackbeard (40-gun *Queen Anne's Revenge*), Black Bart Roberts (42-gun *Royal Fortune*), and Henry Every (46-gun *Fancy*). Not only are these larger vessels far more seaworthy and stable in higher seas, they also provide a platform for more great guns and a larger crew, making it easier to overpower wealthy merchantmen and East Indian galleons whose holds are always chock-full of valuable cargo.

Some pirate captains prefer to expand their influence with each prize they capture by creating, and subsequently adding to, a fleet of pirate ships. In most cases, the captain will appoint his quartermaster to command the newly acquired prize to sail in consort with the flagship, creating an overwhelming—and often deadly—experience for the next prey ship they encounter. A few examples:

1. 1671, when Henry Morgan sailed from Port Royal, Jamaica, to sack and plunder Panama, his fleet consisted of thirty-seven vessels, ranging from 4-gunners to 22-gunners.

New Providence

Twenty-eight miles long and eleven miles wide, the Bahamian colony of New Providence is the ultimate pirate playground. Its natural harbor can shelter up to five hundred ships with anchorages at least thirty feet deep. However, because there is a sandbar leading in to the island, access is denied to pirate-hunting warships. A large market offers every available commodity or provision, and, for piratical fun and games, there are plenty of brothels, gaming houses, taverns, and grog shops. It is said that when a pirate slept, he didn't dream that he'd died and gone to heaven, he dreamed that he had once again returned to New Providence.

They don't call it "no prey, no pay" for nothin'.

STEDE BONNET, the "gentleman pirate," should have followed the leads of Henry Every and Thomas Tew before going on account. In 1717, Bonnet, with more money than brains, actually purchased and outfitted a 10-gun sloop—which he named *Revenge*—and then went so far as to pay seventy men to crew her. This wimpy approach to privateering backfired big time when the legendary Blackbeard caught up with ol' Stede and forced him and his crew to sail under his flag.

Always take advantage of what Mother Nature gives you.

In 1715, a dozen Spanish treasure ships were caught in the horror of a hurricane and driven into the reefs fringing Florida's eastern shore. The Spanish wasted no time in sending out rescue parties and salvage crews to retrieve the sunken silver. **CAPTAIN HENRY JENNINGS** recruited a force of three hundred pirates with a plan to relieve the Spanish of their prize cargo. Jennings anchored his four ships out of sight of the Spanish fort and the salvage operation. As darkness descended, Jennings's crew ambushed the fort, forcing the retreat of the Spanish soldiers, and the pirates walked away with more than 350,000 pesos.

NEVER LET AN OPPORTUNITY PASS.

In 1668, **ROBERT SEARLES** (a.k.a. John Davis) captured Pierre Piquet, a French surgeon who had just sailed out of St. Augustine, Florida, after being fired by Spanish Governor Francisco de la Guerra. In the spirit of revenge, Piquet revealed some tasty information to Captain Searles: Silver bars had been recovered from the wreck of a treasure ship and were being held in the St. Augustine presidio. Under the guise of a Spanish supply ship, Searles sailed into the harbor and unleashed his barbarous crew on the presidio, killing sixty citizens and stealing the booty.

Here we had news of a peace concluded between the Spaniards and the Indians of Darien, who are commonly at war one with the other. This made us agree to visit the said place, and in order thereto dispersed our selves into several coves, there to careen and fit our vessels for that purpose. Here, at Boca del Toro, we found plenty of fat tortoises, the pleasantest meat in the world. Our vessels being refitted, we rendezvouz'd at an island, called by us, the Water-Key, and our strength was as followeth.

	TUNS	GUNS	MEN
CAPT. COXON IN A SHIP OF	80	8	97
CAPT. HARRIS IN ANOTHER OF	150	25	107
CAPT. BOURNAMO	90	6	86
CAPT. SAWKINS	16	1	35
CAPT. SHARP	25	2	40
CAPT. COOK	35	0	43
CAPT. ALLESTON	18	0	24
CAPT. ROW	20	0	25
CAPT. MACKET	14	0	20

BASIL RINGROSE, *The Dangerous Voyage and Bold Attempts of Capt. Barth. Sharp, Watlin, Sawkins, Coxon, and Others, in the South Sea* (**1684**)

2. 1718, Blackbeard's blockade of Charleston utilized four ships: the 40-gun *Queen Anne's Revenge*, the 10-gun *Adventure*, and two smaller sloops armed with six and eight guns respectively.

3. 1721, Black Bart Roberts commanded a fleet of four vessels: the 42-gun *Royal Fortune*, the 32-gun *Great Ranger*, the 30-gun *Sea King*, and a 16-gun sloop.

Despite their advantages, larger pirate ships also have their drawbacks. Because of their size, there is a scarcity of ports where they can dock, and even fewer safe shores where they can be beached and careened. And since the deep-drafted vessels cannot hide up rivers or within inlets as can shallow-drafted sloops, they have to be manned at all times, with a watch crew left on deck while the rest of the crew goes ashore for fun and plunder, oftentimes fostering an air of resentment and dissent among those who stay behind to mind the store.

bring to!

CHAPTER
EIGHT

Ship-Shape Speed

*"Had you fought like a man,
you need not be hanged like a dog."*

—

Anne Bonny

Without question, the ship is the most important tool in the pirate's repertoire. Not only does it serve as our home—a floating, mobile domicile—it is also the means by which we earn a living. Bottom line: Pirates' survival depends almost entirely upon the ship. Therefore, the vessel needs to be fast, agile, and, above all else, durable. And it also needs to perform optimally at all times, regardless of weather conditions or circumstances. Keep in mind that piracy isn't always about combat. Sometimes, the smarter course of action is leaving conflict in your wake, for he who fights and runs away lives to fight (and plunder) another day. As such, anything compromising a pirate ship's flawless (or near flawless) function needs to be handled posthaste.

When repairs inside the ship—either on or below decks—are needed, the captain will mobilize as many crewmen as possible to remedy the problem(s) expeditiously without taking away from the vessel's current operation. Exterior repairs, however, are a whole different kettle of fish.

Above-the-waterline troubles are easy enough to fix when the ship is anchored or moored. On the move, these same repairs become a bit more challenging, but, via the use of ropes (safety tethers) and planks (seated workstations), they can usually be handled without too much difficulty or excessive danger. It's the ship's dilemmas *beneath* the waves—on the hull—that give all those aboard pits in their guts the size of Jamaica.

To carry out below-the-waterline repairs, sailors must rely on a combination of their physical environment, the whims of Mother Nature, and their own ingenuity. For ships away from their home ports—especially pirate ships, which usually have no home port to speak of—this involves a process known as *careening*.

Besides being physically arduous, careening, while absolutely necessary from time to time to keep our vessels afloat and ship-shape (fast, agile, safe), creates a scenario of extreme danger for the crew because the ship is immobile and defenseless throughout the process, akin to a turtle on its back.

[FIG. 28] CAREENING

To successfully careen a ship, the captain will first sail her to a deserted island, secret harbor, or, in the absence of the aforementioned, a coral reef or sandbar—somewhere well away from shipping lanes and any other heavily trafficked areas. Here, the crew will offload the necessities to survive on land. Barrels of water (if there is no freshwater source on the island within easy reach), grog, and salted meat are all hoisted from the hold using a *block-and-tackle*. Weapons—from small arms to cannons and their implements (gunpowder, cannonballs, fuse)—along with spare masts and ballast stones are also removed from the ship to set up a secure land-based defensive battery in the event of attack by an enemy ship stumbling onto the careening locale. Everything else left on board the ship is lashed down tightly to protect it from damage.

Next, at high tide, the ship is sailed aground onto the remote beach or sandbar and anchored or tethered into place. Then, at low tide, it is gently flopped onto its side like a beached whale, once again using block-and-tackles or, in the absence of pulleys, the muscle of the crew holding ropes wound around a tree (or trees) as an assist to control the momentum. Because time is of the essence—the longer the ship is laid up, the greater the danger—the crew will spring into action, ridding the hull of barnacles and other swiftness-inhibiting sea growth with hammers and scraping irons. Rotten timbers are replaced, and any gaps between planks are caulked or filled with *oakum* before being shellacked with a mixture of tallow, oil, and brimstone. After the shellac dries, a final coating of resinous amber-colored tar (made from pine tree sap) is applied for further protection.

After one side of the ship has been completed, the ship is then flipped to the other side and the procedure repeated. Although the crew works carefully, they also work hastily, for every day the ship is incapacitated is another day without pay. Remember, we live by a simple motto: *No prey, no pay.*

BLOCK-AND-TACKLE

A pulley system used to lift heavy loads.

ROGUE STRATEGY

How to Set Up an Island Battery

. The island battery should be positioned to protect the anchored/careened pirate ship. Off-loaded cannons need to be close enough to be within range of potential enemy ships; cliffs and mouths of inlets or rivers are perfect for this.

. Areas defensible from all sides, allowing for 360-degree protection, are excellent island battery locales.

. Places that cannot be seen by approaching enemy ships until it's too late—when they are within range of the big guns—are ideal for island battery ambushes.

. Pirates don't like to be surprised, but they love to surprise attack!

[FIG. 29] ISLAND BATTERY

SHIP REPAIR

OAKUM
A preparation of old rope fibers covered in pine tar.

RAMMING IRON
A broad-bladed tool used for splitting open rotten seams.

JERRY IRON
The angled blade is specifically designed to chop out old oakum from inside seams.

CAULKING IRON
With its narrow blade, this tool is perfect for driving new oakum into seams.

PITCH LADLE
This ladle's funneled tip is designed for pouring hot pitch into seams.

Aside from emergency repairs for damage inflicted during battle, the careening process is carried out approximately twice a year, especially when the vessel spends the bulk of its time in warm tropical waters where clingy, aerodynamic-hampering sea life (barnacles, algae, and the like) flourish. The dreaded *teredo worms*—a.k.a. sea termites, miniscule saltwater clams that feast on wood and bore holes through planks—also factor considerably into the need to careen. And then there are the heavy seas and powerful wind torque, constant natural forces that contort the ship every nautical mile it sails, causing planks to bulge and seams to split. Pirates are well aware that no ship, no matter how sturdily built, will stay afloat if the sea is invited along for the ride.

While island batteries are usually set up solely for defensive purposes, they can also be formidably offensive. In 1686, following the capture of two English ships off the coast of Caracas, Joseph Bannister sailed to the northeastern side of Hispaniola to careen his ship, *Golden Fleece*, in the bay of Samana. While readying for repairs, the crew clandestinely off-loaded several of her big guns and formed defensive batteries ashore. Shortly thereafter, the HMS *Drake* and the HMS *Falcon* sailed into Samana searching for Bannister. A ferocious clash of cannon fire ensued, lasting from three in the afternoon until well into the following evening, when the frigates' guns exhausted their powder supplies. With twenty-three men killed and wounded, the Royal Navy ships reluctantly limped away. Although the *Golden Fleece* was a wreck, Bannister and his crew were fit to fight another day.

What happens when you don't set up an island battery? Nothing good. In 1722, while careening his ship, *Happy Delivery*, on a small island northeast of Tortuga, George Lowther and his crew were surprised by the HMS *Eagle*, commanded by Walter Moore. Those pirates who weren't killed were captured and condemned to death at St. Kitts. Captain Lowther was later found dead on the beach.

REMOVING BARNACLES (AND OTHER CLINGY SEA LIFE) FROM A SHIP WITHOUT DAMAGING THE HULL

- When using hammers or scraping irons, be sure to strike barnacles at a sharp angle—the sharper, the better. Straight downward strikes are more likely to cause damage to the ship's surface, as are drunken pirates, so be sure to keep the tools out of their hands!

- Wood planks, held lengthwise in both hands, can be used as scraping agents, mitigating the damage metal tools might cause to the ship.

- The warmer the water, the faster barnacles and other clingy sea life will accumulate. Also, the longer a ship remains motionless, the easier it is for growths to form.

- The longer buildup is allowed to accumulate, the harder it will be to remove.

THE SHIP AIN'T GONNA FIX ITSELF!

Besides a navigator, a skilled carpenter is an absolute necessity aboard a ship. The carpenter, with his trusty bag of tools, is an invaluable part of the careening process, and, because he also pulls double-duty as the ship's surgeon, he is equally handy for dealing with the crew's post-battle wounds. When **CAPTAIN HOWELL DAVIS** beached his ship, *Rover*, on the eastern shores of Cuba for a much-needed careening, it was immediately discovered that he forgot to recruit a carpenter. This lack of expertise delayed the process considerably and damn near cost him and his crew their lives. Shortly thereafter, the crew removed Davis from the captaincy.

St. Mary's Island

CAPTAIN KIDD, **THOMAS TEW**, **HENRY EVERY**, and **ROBERT CULLIFORD** all used the little island off the east coast of Madagascar to careen their ships. St. Mary's Island (a.k.a. Coconut Island), actually a set of four small islands, is ideally suited for this purpose for many reasons. For one, its location makes it the perfect stopover for pirates raiding the Great Mogul's ships in the Indian Ocean. It's also a mainstay on every pirate captain's charts because of its numerous hidden bays and inlets, ample forests for much-needed timber, an abundance of fresh fruit, and other life-sustaining supplies.

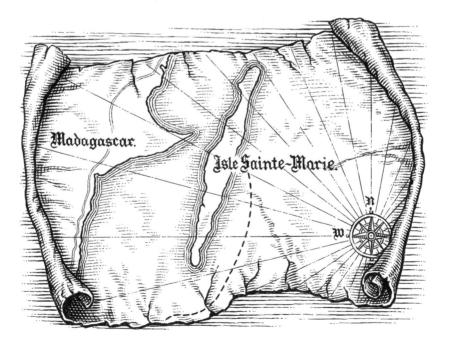

[FIG. 30] MAP OF ST. MARY'S ISLAND

LAND
HO!

"Nobody but the devil and I
know where the treasure is,
and the longest liver shall have it all."

—

BLACKBEARD

*P*irates spend the bulk of their time at sea, aboard their ships, searching for prizes to plunder. However, they also spend quite a bit of time ashore, pillaging towns and settlements, setting up defensive batteries, careening their vessels, or simply seeking some R & R, although the piratical version of rest and relaxation consists of running amok and raising a tankard. As such, pirates have to be capable of surviving on land as well. And considering that rogues usually scatter like cockroaches in sunlight the moment their feet hit sand or dock—in search of the nearest brothel, tavern, or gaming house—that means an abundance of solo scenarios with nary an armed-to-the-teeth crewmate or ship's big guns to bail them out of trouble when they find it. And trust me, pirates find trouble *a lot!* Bottom line: Pirates need to be able to fend for themselves, wherever they are.

Once ashore, finding shelter for the night is usually the second order of business; when you're a pirate, fun always comes first! After sleeping in cramped, squalid, smelly confines for lengthy periods of time, anything other than the eighteen- to twenty-four-inch-wide impersonal shipboard space of a hammock is a welcome change. Still, the shelter has to provide some sort of protection from the elements, insects, and wild animals—and potentially from other wandering rogues.

Finding a hut or a similar dwelling and "evicting" its owner or current occupant is the easiest method—remember, pirates are bad-asses, not churchgoers—but the simpler (and far safer) method is building your own. Considering that pirates spend most of their time in tropical environments, a lean-to is the best way to go.

Lean-tos are easy to erect and can be made with virtually any available materials in any locale. And while a lean-to will never offer the same level of protection as a traditional four-walled, fixed-roof structure, the amount of protection a lean-to provides can mean the difference between a fitful night of sleep and none at all.

CARIBBEAN ISLANDS

The vast majority of islands in the Caribbean have at least one source of freshwater and more than enough food—fish, game, and plant life—to support pirates for any length of time. Considering that there are more than seven thousand islands, islets, and cays in this geographical area, pirates have plenty of shore excursions to choose from.

ALL PLUNDER AND NO PLAY MAKES FOR DULL PIRATES!

In September of 1718, following months of successful plundering raids, the crews of **BLACKBEARD** and **CHARLES VANE** rendezvoused on Ocracoke Island (North Carolina) for a wild, no-holds-barred bacchanal. With both crews saluting themselves and each other for more than a week, it's safe to assume that more than a bit of rum was consumed, and more than a few moments of debauchery took place.

We hunted generally in the daytimes, killing black cattle, hogs, etc. for the substance, and in the night retired to our tents and huts, sometimes when the weather grew cold.

CAPTAIN CHARLES JOHNSON,
A General History of the Pyrates (1726)

BUILDING A LEAN-TO

1 Find a dry area with plenty of drainage. If on the beach, make sure you select a spot well above the high-tide mark.

2 Be aware of wind direction; the back of your lean-to should offer protection from the wind.

3 Gather a pile of branches, the straighter and sturdier (thicker) the better.

4 Place two branches in the ground vertically. A rooted tree can also be used as one of the supports.

5 Place another branch between the two upright branches, making a crossbar. You can cut notches into the ends of the branches for a more secure fit, or simply break off pieces, leaving your support branches with Y-shaped ends.

6 Lay additional branches diagonally, from the crossbar to the ground. The more, the better.

7 Vines or softer live branches can be used as connectors, interwoven between the frame branches.

8 Insert large leaves or, better yet, palm fronds between the frame branches, making the weave as tight as possible to protect from wind and rain.

9 Start at the bottom and work your way up. Overlap as you get higher. Your top layer should be the outermost, allowing water to run down smoothly.

10 If on a slope, a hand-dug drainage groove will help carry away rainwater runoff more efficiently.

11 Using the softest foliage possible, create a sleeping mat under the lean-to. Be sure and check foliage for insects first. "Smoking" the area/foliage with a torch is a good way to get rid of insects or creepy-crawlies that may bite or sting.

12 A nearby fire can be utilized for this same purpose.

13 Force a prisoner or an unliked crewman to do most/all of the work and then get rid of him.

[FIG. 31] LEAN-TO

MAKE A HAMMOCK

1 Gather your materials. For the body of the hammock, a piece of sailcloth (or fish netting) is ideal, approximately three feet wide by two feet longer than the user's height.

2 Acquire thirty to fifty feet of strong, non-stretchable rope, cut into two equal lengths.

3 Tie a strong knot at each end of the fabric.

4 Fold one length of rope in half and tie a knot in the middle, creating a looped end with two separate strands.

5 Repeat this step with the other length of rope.

6 Wrap the looped end of rope around the first anchor point (tree trunk, tree branch, railing, etc.), then pass one end of the loop through the other and cinch it tightly.

7 Put your right hand through the bottom of the extending loop of rope and grasp the two dangling strands; the loop should rest on the back of your forearm. Using your left hand, lift the loop over your right hand to create a movable loop that will support your hammock.

8 Slip one knotted end of hammock material through the movable loop of rope and slide the rope down around the knot.

9 Repeat the preceding three steps for the other end of the hammock.

10 Spread the hammock material and apply firm, even pressure to test its strength. If it holds, climb in and get some rest.

11 Once again, don't do the work yourself. Force someone else to do it then scare him away with a dagger, cutlass, or flintlock.

Undisturbed rest is an invaluable commodity for anyone, especially pirates, and it is extremely difficult to come by aboard a ship. Sleeping on deck, under the stars, is an option but is not very comfortable. Below deck, the floor is the last place a pirate wants to bed down; rats, refuse, sewage, and seawater are just a few hazards one might encounter. Thus, on land as at sea, hammocks are the answer. They take up very little room, can be mounted virtually anywhere, hardly ever break—they swing/flex with the movements of the ship—and can be fashioned by just about anyone with even the barest of essentials. So when it comes to sleeping ashore, hammocks are once again the most sensible option, if for no other reason than the fact that pirates are already familiar with their construction. An added bonus: They keep you off the ground, away from the innumerable creepy-crawlies (snakes, spiders, ants, land crabs, etc.) that scurry about the islands at night.

From a survival standpoint, fire should be your next order of business, although depending on the time of day (or night), making a fire will often be the first priority.

Fire has been linked to human survival since man first walked upright. From providing warmth, to cooking food, to warding off critters and insects, to simply lifting spirits, fire is a physical and psychological necessity, and pirates can often be found congregating around campfires on the beach long after they've left the bordellos and rum taverns.

Most pirates carry the proper tools to start a fire quickly—namely black powder or an oil lantern, along with a match or a flintlock pistol. But in a pinch—occasionally even the most well-equipped pirates find themselves without proper fire-making implements—the ancient concept of *friction* (produced by rubbing two objects together) can be relied upon.

For friction to result in fire, at least two pieces of dry wood are required. And while there are numerous methods for creating flame from nature's bounty, the best and most efficient is the *spindle and bow.*

[FIG. 32] MAKING A FIRE

ROGUE STRATEGY

MAKING FIRE VIA SPINDLE AND BOW

Four pieces of wood are required:

#1 **THE BOW** should be two to three feet long and one inch thick, tied with a piece of strong twine.

#2 **THE SPINDLE** should be about one foot long and one inch thick, rounded at one end, formed into a blunt point at the other. You will push the rounded end into . . .

#3 **THE SOCKET BOARD**, a palm-size piece of wood used to hold the spindle in place while bowing. Use grease or sweat on the rounded end of the spindle, allowing it to move easily in the socket board. Finally, place the blunt point of the spindle into . . .

#4 **THE FIREBOARD**, which is roughly one foot long, three to six inches wide, and a quarter-inch thick.

IN ONE END of the fireboard, carve a small hole and cut a V-shaped notch with the opening at the edge, pointing at the hollow. Wood shavings from your bowing will collect here and, from the heat produced via friction, become charcoal dust. If done correctly, in the center of that dust will be a hot ember. Once you have your utensils and a relatively wind- and rain-free place to work, begin bowing:

1 Place the fireboard on the ground, either atop two small sticks or in a dry hollow to ensure airflow.

2 Place tinder under the fireboard, beneath the V-cut.

3 Twist the bowstring once around the spindle.

4 Place the blunt end of the spindle into the notch on the fireboard and the rounded end into the socket board. Using long, even strokes, twist the spindle back and forth vigorously until smoke is produced.

5 Continue bowing, creating thicker smoke. If done properly, the charcoal dust collected in the V-cut can be rolled off the fireboard onto the waiting tinder.

6 The dust should now be hot enough so that if lightly blown upon, a glowing ember will appear. As the ember's glow increases, gently pick up your tinder and continue blowing to create a flame.

7 Place the flaming tinder onto your preassembled kindling and slowly feed the fire with small, dry twigs and other combustible items until it is large enough to handle a branch or log.

8 Because this process is far from easy and is extremely time-consuming, think ahead and always have some type of fire-making implement available.

9 Be sure to build your fire away from water, wind zones, and combustibles, especially your newly constructed lean-to.

Before you get started with the spindle and bow (or any fire-making method, for that matter), you should first assemble your entire fire-making "kit."

Gathering *tinder* is the first step. Paper, saw dust, wood shavings, dry bark—any small, light material with a low flash point will work. This is what you light first.

Lit tinder is then placed into a prearranged formation of *kindling*—smaller pieces of wood (dry twigs, dry pinecones, dry coconut husks) that catch fire easily. Kindling should be assembled into a framework of sorts; a small "teepee" is ideal because smoldering tinder can be placed inside it, and air will easily feed the flames.

Once the kindling has taken and produced a small, consistent fire, *fuel* can be added. Dead, dry branches, grass bundles, logs, dry dung—any larger material that will burn (and burn for a while) can be considered. Keep plenty on hand to make certain the fire burns throughout the night. The last thing any pirate wants to do is start tromping around in the darkness—especially if he's foggy from rum—looking for something to burn. Too many dangers lurk about on islands at night, the top two being pirate hunters and other pirates!

While fire is a nice luxury, it isn't an essential element for survival. Water, however, most certainly is. You can survive for a few weeks without food—granted, you'll be a weak pirate, but still among the living—but you can only last a few days without water.

Some pirates discover this the hard way. Shipboard barrels of water are prized commodities. When pirates plunder their prey, water barrels are among the first booty they search for, right up there with rum barrels. And when rain isn't prevalent, more than a few ships detour from their merchant-shipping lane "hunting grounds" to the nearest group of islands to replenish their stocks of life-sustaining freshwater.

When pirates go ashore, especially on an unfamiliar or previously uncharted island, if they are planning on staying for any length of time, scouts are immediately dispatched to locate a freshwater source. Most islands have at least one, although some are bleak and barren and, therefore, not hospitable for more than a day or so (depending on the ship's remaining supplies). No matter where you are, or what terrain you're traversing, there are a few commonalities that can help you find water.

ANIMAL TRACKS. Animals require water just as humans do. A heavy concentration of tracks (a game trail, for example) can be followed and, sooner or later, the tracks should lead to a water source.

HEAVY CONCENTRATION OF PLANTS. An abundance of plant life in any given area generally indicates the presence of surface water and/or an underground aquifer. If there are thick clumps of green, water is close by.

SWARMING INSECTS. Insects congregate to drink, especially at dusk. Bees, dragonflies, mosquitoes, and ants are the best types to watch, as they can lead you directly to a water source.

BIRDS. Watch where they flock. If you don't locate a water source you may find a nesting site that will provide you with food (eggs or baby birds).

VALLEY FLOORS. If no visible water source can be found, find the lowest point on a valley floor and start digging along the sloping sides to find water.

As soon as a freshwater source is discovered, you'll need to determine if it's safe to drink. If it's discolored, has a foul smell, contains dead animals or animal skeletons, has foam, or has a high salinity (or a high amount of crusting around it), chances are the source has serious problems. If you're in doubt, force a prisoner or the least-liked crewman to sample it. Then wait a few minutes. If he doesn't start to claw at his throat, or simply keel over and die, drink up.

If the water is not drinkable, most pirates (at least the sober ones) are smart enough to take the proper steps to make it so. Otherwise, healthy pirates will quickly become sick pirates. And in most cases, sick pirates will soon become dead pirates.

Boiling water is the easiest method of purification. Simply make a fire, boil the water for ten minutes or so, let it cool, and drink. If you can't boil water, then you're probably not a very good pirate and you deserve to die anyway. But just in case there's a good reason why a pirate such as you *can't* boil water, here are a few additional methods for making it safe to drink:

SEDIMENT HOLE: Instead of drinking water directly from the source (stream, lake, river, valley floor, etc.), dig a small hole a few feet away and allow it to fill with water. Although the water may initially appear cloudy, it will be sufficiently filtered to allow safe consumption.

FILTRATION TOWER: A filtration tower is a manmade, tri-level tripod device composed of sticks and any porous cloth. The top level of cloth contains grasses; the middle level holds fine-grain sand; and the bottom level holds charcoal.

1. Place a mug or flask below level three.

2. Pour water into the top layer of grass, allowing it to filter down through all the levels.

3. Collected water has been filtered of larger contaminates, however microscopic organisms may still be present.

DISTILLATION: This method involves a still. A basic still can be made with two containers and a tube.

1. Place one end of a tube into the container of liquid to be distilled (in this case, water), and the other end into an empty collection container.

Producing Water by Hook or by Crook

If you're stranded (or marooned) and cannot locate any freshwater sources, you may be able to produce some.

DEW RAG
In the morning, use a shirt, bandana, or any other moisture-absorbing cloth to soak up morning dew.

RAIN RAG
When it's raining, tie a cloth around a slightly slanted tree or bush, allowing one end to hang freely into a container or, if thirsty, your mouth. Cloth will serve as a funnel, guiding rainwater into the container, as well as accumulating in the cloth itself. If no cloth is available, a thick palm frond will work.

Mosquito Protection

Mosquitoes are a very real problem for pirates while doing all kinds of things like sneaking into native encampments to steal gold or waiting in ambush just inside the tree line of tropical islands or jungles for unsuspecting prey. Anything that can be done to minimize their annoying and disease-carrying bites is worth doing.

- **COVERING** extremities in fabric will decrease areas mosquitoes can attack.
- **CEDAR SHAVINGS** are a natural insect repellent for tents, debris huts, and lean-tos.
- **RUB** crushed cedar needles onto your skin.
- If cedar needles are unavailable, a thin coating of **MUD** will also work.
- **SMOKE** from a torch or campfire will also ward off mosquitoes.
- **SMUDGE FIRES** (fires fueled with leaves and green wood) produce extra smoke.
- **AVOID** areas of heavily concentrated standing/stagnant water.

2. Heat the filled container until it boils.

3. The produced vapor will enter the tube, where it will cool and condense, filling the collection container with clean, drinkable water. This method can be used on both sea-water and urine.

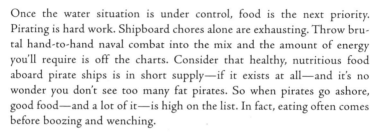

Once the water situation is under control, food is the next priority. Pirating is hard work. Shipboard chores alone are exhausting. Throw brutal hand-to-hand naval combat into the mix and the amount of energy you'll require is off the charts. Consider that healthy, nutritious food aboard pirate ships is in short supply—if it exists at all—and it's no wonder you don't see too many fat pirates. So when pirates go ashore, good food—and a lot of it—is high on the list. In fact, eating often comes before boozing and wenching.

Just like with shelter (and water, for that matter), finding people who already have food and simply taking it from them is definitely the piratical way. It's certainly much easier, not to mention more fun. But if you and your crewmates are the only inhabitants on the island, you'll have to fend for yourselves.

Finding food in the wild is a challenging undertaking. Mounds of delicious edibles aren't just sitting around, waiting for you to happen by. This means snaring, trapping, and hunting. The first step is to determine what game is in the area so you can decide the best way to go about capturing, killing, and eating it. Identifying animal tracks is the best approach. Not only will a hungry pirate know what to look for, but, by following the tracks, you'll discover the best place to lay in wait for your prey.

Hunting with flintlock or musket is the quickest method, especially for large game, but before you can shoot it, you have to find it, and that's easier said than done. To save time and increase your chances of success, snares and traps are often the best game-taking method to employ. Once the traps are set, you can busy yourself with other tasks—erecting a shelter, building a fire, or purifying water—while the traps do what they're designed for.

Snares—devices made of twine/rope, fabricated into a lasso/noose, and secured to a rock or tree—are most effective when placed along a well-traveled game trail or near a heavily frequented watering hole. A *simple snare* consists of a lasso placed in a well-traveled area. A *dynamic snare* is tied to a bent sapling or tree and held with a trigger mechanism—usually a stick; when the animal is caught, the snare hoists it off the ground, making escape much more difficult. Some dynamic snares are powerful enough to snap the animal's neck or smack it onto the ground or against a hard surface with killing force.

SIMPLE SNARES

1. Place along well-used game trails, by water sources, or near active nests and burrows.

2. Make sure loop is large enough for your targeted prey, but not too large to allow escape.

3. Bait snare with entrails or any other odorous foodstuff.

DYNAMIC SNARES

1. Attach trigger mechanism—a notched stick—so a minimum amount of force will set it in motion.

2. Tied rope or line should be just strong enough to hold bent tree/sapling down; if too tight it may not trigger.

3. Carefully bait snare after it's been set.

4. Remember exact placement of your snares so you don't become caught in them yourself.

In truth, the best trap to take the time to build and set is one that can be employed against your enemies as well, such as a pitfall trap, especially in the proximity of any treasure you've buried.

PITFALL TRAP

1. Dig a pit, ideally at least three times deeper than the target species is tall.

2. Line pit with sharp spikes. Wooden *punji* stakes are best.

3. Bait pit on opposite side of the target's expected direction of approach. If your quarry is a pirate-hunter or another pirate, a gold or silver doubloon, a bottle of rum, or a pretty lass makes for great bait.

4. Conceal the opening with branches and shrubbery.

5. Remember where you put the trap or you might trap yourself.

Though hunting game is a bonus when you go ashore, fish are a much more common part of the pirate diet, whether on ship or on land. Fish are prevalent around all tropical islands; fishing with hook and line accounts for many a meal, but spearing them is much easier.

However, if you strike out on both surf and turf, there are always plants and insects to consider. But just like with making fire, if you're a real pirate, you won't strike out. After all, you're not going to satisfy your appetite eating bugs or greens.

Cooking your acquired fish or game is easily accomplished without traditional implements. Virtually every common cooking method—boiling, steaming, parching, roasting, and frying—can be achieved in the field with a little ingenuity.

For **BOILING,** a metal pot placed over or near a fire works just fine. Or use a stone with a deep depression, provided the stone doesn't have a high moisture content, in which case it can explode, sending rock shards flying like shrapnel. A hollow log will also work, as will turtle and coconut shells, and bamboo sections.

STEAMING is achieved by putting hot coals at the bottom of a manmade pit. Cover the coals with moss or leaves, then place the food—wrapped inside large leaves (banana leaves or palm fronds are ideal) or in a bundle of smaller leaves—on top and bury. Leave a small hole for airflow to keep the coals smoldering. Dig it up in a little while and dig in.

PARCHING—most effective for drying earthworms, insects, and some plants—is best accomplished by placing a large, flat rock near a fire; the rock heats up, slowly heating and drying the food.

ROASTING is the best method for most meats, whether gutted, skinned, and skewered, or, for fish, gutted and cooked whole.

FRYING is best saved for eggs, using a flat, low-moisture rock beside a fire.

After pirates' basic needs are met, the remainder of shore time is spent gambling, chasing lasses, and drinking, not necessarily in that order. Gambling is customary among pirates and, naturally, some are better at it than others. Because there isn't much time for leisure activities aboard the ship, pirates usually have to wait until they go ashore to cut loose. Not only that, gambling is strictly prohibited on most pirate vessels—with harsh penalties for those who disobey the signed Articles—so games of chance are usually reserved for land. Before engaging in any games with

How to Make a Fish Spear

1 Find a long, straight branch or cut a straight sapling seven to eight feet long and approximately one broom-handle thick.

2 Slice one end of the branch/sapling down the center approximately four to six inches deep.

3 Insert a piece of wood into the cut to keep the two halves split apart.

4 Lash wedge with rope/line/sinew to keep prongs from separating further.

5 Sharpen prongs.

6 Notch a barb in one or both prongs (optional) to prevent fish from sliding off.

7 If using live wood, fire-harden prongs by inserting into flame.

8 Remember to aim a few inches below the fish, just behind its gill plate.

9 Don't throw the spear. Instead, make a fast, smooth jab.

[FIG. 33] SPEAR FISHING

How to Gut a Fish

While it may be fun to drop a fish, especially one with sharp teeth or barbs, down a prisoner's trousers, you're better off killing it immediately. Handling a live, flopping fish with fins, spines, razor-sharp gill plates, and teeth can be dangerous. Brain it with a dagger or sharp stick, bash its head with a rock, or smack its head on the ground.

1 Slit fish from its anus to its gills.

2 Pull out innards. Save these for additional bait and traps.

3 Wash and clean fish inside and out.

4 Cut down to the spine (but don't cut through it), then cut along both sides of the spine, from tail to gills.

5 Using your thumb and forefinger, grab along the top of the spine and pull up and out. This will leave you with two filets.

6 Option #2 is to simply remove innards and skewer or roast whole, over an open flame.

How to Cook a Snake
(and Other Reptiles)

1 First, decapitate and bury the head. If poisonous, even a severed head can deliver a lethal dose.

2 Slowly pull snakeskin down the body as if you were removing a lass's leggings. This will leave skin intact while simultaneously gutting snake.

3 Skin can be used as a water tube, pouch, or article of clothing.

4 Twist skinned snake around stick and roast over open flame; do not consume until thoroughly cooked. When in doubt, cook longer.

5 Lizards should be gutted, skewered, and roasted until skin splits.

- -

Beaning a Bird
(Or How to Cook a Wild Turkey)

1 A flintlock or musket loaded with shot is best for procuring fowl.

2 In the absence of a firearm, use a throwing device, ideally a hunting stick (throw-able club). A dagger or handful of rocks will also work.

3 Look for birds feeding on the ground, aim just above their heads, and throw. Your movement should cause the birds to alight, hopefully into the path of your projectile(s).

4 Using your hands or a shirt, grab the stunned bird, being sure to control its wings to prevent escape.

5 Holding the head between your thumb and forefinger, swing the bird forcefully in a 360-degree arc to break its neck quickly.

6 For floating/swimming birds (ducks, geese, swans, etc.), swim beneath them, grab by the legs, and pull under. Kill via drowning or breaking its neck.

7 If hunting waterfowl look for nearby nests—usually hidden amid tall reeds—to gather eggs.

8 Once bird is killed, pluck or burn off feathers.

9 Cut from anus to breastbone and remove innards; heart, liver, and kidneys can all be eaten and are an excellent source of protein and vitamins.

10 Skewer and roast over open flame or boil with herbs and vegetables.

your hard-earned plunder or valuable personal items on the line, practice up. And remember, pirates play for keeps. So if you can cheat and get away with it, do it! Here's a list of favorite pirate games:

LIAR´S DICE. Brought back from South America to Spain by famed Spanish conqueror Francisco Pizarro. The game can be played as *Common Hand* or *Individual Hand* versions. It ultimately became very popular with pirates.

COMMON HAND LIAR´S DICE. Each player has a set of five dice. All players roll one and make bids on the dice they can see, along with those they can't.

INDIVIDUAL HAND LIAR´S DICE. One set of dice is passed between players and bids relate to dice in front of the roller/ bidder, including any dice chosen to be re-rolled.

WHIST. This trick-taking card game is a derivative of *Trump* (also called *Ruff*) developed during the sixteenth century. A deck of fifty-two cards—ranking two through ace—is used among four people playing in paired opposition.

MUMBLETY-PEG. Also called *Mumbley-peg*, this knife-throwing game, popular among kids, is also played ashore by pirates, throwing razor-sharp daggers instead of wimpy pocketknives. The goal is to throw your dagger as close to the other person's foot as possible. Needless to say, more than a few toes are left behind on sandy beaches.

THIMBLERIG. Also called *Three Shells and a Pea* or simply *The Shell Game*, this game of chance and deception dates back to the Middle Ages and is extremely popular in pirate taverns. Anyone caught cheating at this game—and many are—lose much more than their winnings, but it still can't hurt to try!

Exploring inlets and waterways—often by raft—is another favorite pirate pastime. Pirates are always on the lookout for native settlements whose residents may have worked with gold or silver, or for access to hidden caves that were repositories for stolen/hidden treasure.

Finally, there is little—if any—privacy aboard pirate ships. There are no places on board that are strictly off-limits to crewmembers. Even the captain and officers, who generally have their own quarters, don't have much in the way of hiding places. So when it comes time to hide amassed booty, land (usually an island) is the best place to do it. And while the act of burying treasure is more hype than substance, it does occur from time to time. The smartest pirates—and ultimately those who retire the wealthiest—bury their treasure, along with a few nasty safeguards in place, just to be sure it will be exactly where they left it when the time comes to dig it up. A few tips to keep in mind:

1. Never tell anyone where your treasure is buried. Even your closest friends can become bitter enemies when treasure or money is in the mix.

2. Disinformation works well to throw prospective treasure hunters off the trail. Dummy up a fake map or two and spread a few stories about where your treasure is supposedly hidden, making sure this location is a world away from where the treasure really is.

3. Pitfall traps work well on humans. Leave a coin or a tiny bauble in an easy-to-find location. That'll get the finder's hopes up and their defenses down and, with any luck, will land them at the bottom of your pit.

[FIG. 34] BUILDING A RAFT

BUILDING A LOG RAFT

Whether you're trying to escape from being marooned on a deserted island, looking to explore inner-island canals and waterways, or perhaps just making a mobile fishing/spearfishing platform, a raft is the best way to go.

- -

1. **GATHER** (or cut) ten reasonably straight logs of about the same length (ten to twelve feet) and girth.

2. **ADD** four shorter logs (five to seven feet long) to the supply pile.

3. **POSITION** two of the shorter logs on the ground approximately a foot shorter than the raft's intended overall length. (Ex: If you're using ten-foot logs, lay shorter ends nine feet apart. Deck [long] logs will be perpendicular to these.)

4. **CARVE** curves off the two shorter logs, making tops flat, so longer "deck logs" will rest squarely atop them.

5. **PUT** all deck (long) logs in place, stretching from one of the shorter, notched end logs to the other. You want a tight fit, with little to no movement in between.

6. **CARVE** curves off the two remaining shorter logs and lay them carved side down, on the ends, above the other two smaller logs, effectively creating a "log sandwich."

7. **SECURE** your construction with rope. Lash a rope around each end, tying off at various points on the raft. If you don't have rope, vines will work. If you have enough rope/vine for four ties (one per side), go for it.

8. **CARRY** or roll (atop logs) your raft to water, climb on, cross your fingers that it holds, and float away.

IF YOU CAN'T FIND MY TREASURE, YOU CAN'T STEAL MY TREASURE!

Despite innumerable romantic tales to the contrary, pirates seldom bury their treasure. However, a small portion of **CAPTAIN WILLIAM KIDD'S** plunder was dug up on Gardiner's Island. Prior to his arrest, Kidd had buried some gold and silver, but the majority of his treasure—valued at more than 400,000 pounds—remains a mystery. In May of 1701, an anxious mob 200,000 strong attended Kidd's execution in the hopes he would reveal the exact location. However, Kidd took his secret to the grave.

TREATING SNAKE AND SPIDER BITES

1 Restrict movement; a loose splint will help.

2 If the bite is on the hand or fingers, remove rings or other constricting jewelry.

3 Keep bitten area below heart level to minimize spread of venom.

4 Get medical help as soon as possible.

5 If the ship's surgeon (carpenter) recommends amputation, either drink your fill of rum first or place your dagger or flintlock against the surgeon's throat and get a second opinion!

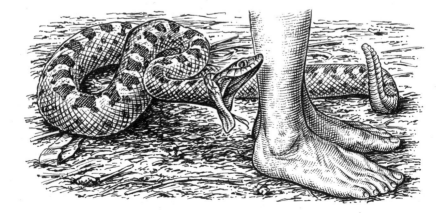

[FIG. 35] SNAKE BITE

Captain Henry Morgan, who knew very well all the avenues of this city, and the neighboring coasts, arriv'd in the dusk of the evening at Puerto de Naos, ten leagues to the west of Puerto Velo. They had in their company an English–man, formerly a prisoner in those parts, who now serv'd them for a guide. To him and three or four more, they gave commission to take the sentry, if possible, or kill him on the place. But they seiz'd him so cunningly as he had no time to give warning with his musket, or make any noise; and brought him, with his bound, to Capt. Morgan, who ask'd him, "How things went in the city, and what forces they had." After every question, they made him a thousand menaces to kill him, if he declar'd not the truth. Then they advanc'd to the city, carrying the said sentry bound before them. Having march'd about a quarter of a league, they came to the castle near the city; which presently they closely surrounded, so that no person could get either in or out.

ALEXANDRE EXQUEMELIN,
Bucaniers of America (1 6 8 4)

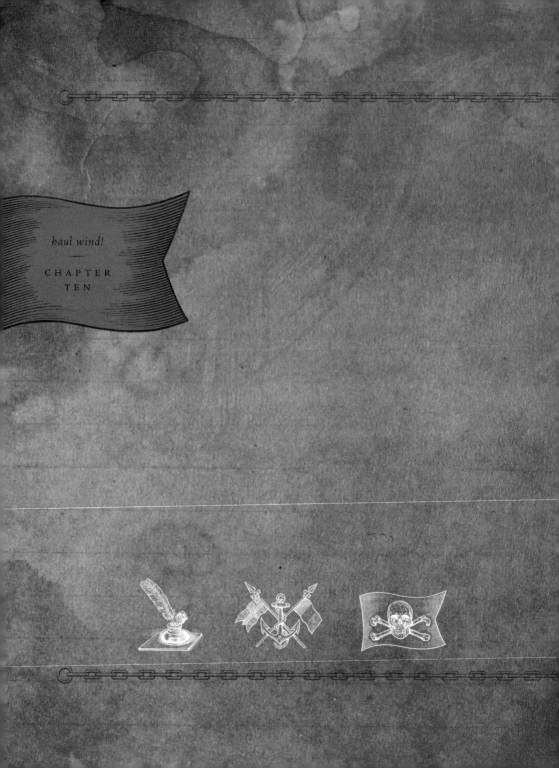

haul wind!

CHAPTER
TEN

TORTURE, RANSOM & PIRATICAL POLITICS

"I have brought you to the treasure house of the world."

—

SIR FRANCIS DRAKE

Aside from our barbarous exploits and over-indulgent tendencies, we pirates—especially the successful among us—are shrewd and cunning businessmen who know how to get things done in all scenarios, under any circumstances. From a longevity standpoint, we also know how to stay alive, stay out of prison, and stay off the execution docks.

Plundering vessels under the black flag—free of any autocratic captains on either land or sea—is what we live for. And should we be so unfortunate as to get caught, hopefully we've had the chance to secure a pardon from a queen, king, or government—the ultimate free pass that forgives all past sins and rescinds any order of imprisonment or execution. Granted, a pardon means we're now indebted to our savior, beholden to fight their enemies wherever we encounter them, but that's a small price to pay when you consider the alternative. However, pardons aren't given out too often.

An example of this favorable treatment was bestowed upon perhaps the most notorious pirate ever to roam the seas—Blackbeard. After plundering merchant ships along the Atlantic seaboard, Blackbeard and his crew would routinely celebrate their windfall with the grateful citizens of North Carolina, allowing them to purchase goods without the customary stiff tariff imposed. It was like getting items from the black market, only in this case it was the Blackbeard market. As a show of thanks for Blackbeard's generosity, Governor Charles Eden granted him a full pardon.

A similar pass from those in charge is the letter of marque, an authorization or commission from a queen, king, or government giving privateers the legal authority to *take action* (search, seize, plunder, and/or destroy) against the ships of their enemies. William Kidd, captain of the *Adventure Galley*, received a letter of marque from King William III to seize any French ships encountered during his search for pirates in the Indian Ocean. Kidd believed his acts of piracy were legitimate privateering conquests and, therefore, lawful seizures. In a similar case, pirate Jean Lafitte

[FIG. 36] WILLIAM KIDD

[FIG. 37] MADAME CHING

HE WHO LIVES WITH THE MOST BOOTY WINS!

WOODES ROGERS sailed into the New Providence pirate stronghold in 1718 with a fleet of four Royal Navy warships, bringing a pardon direct from King George I for all pirates who turned themselves in and promised to refrain from further piratical activities. The alternative was a final dance at the end of an admiralty rope. **BENJAMIN HORNIGOLD** happily complied with the terms and was permitted to keep all of his ill-gotten gains—and his life.

With the death of her pirate husband, Zheng Yi, in 1807, former prostitute **CHING SHIH** (a.k.a. Madame Ching) took command of a pirate fleet of four hundred junks, extorting protection payments throughout the South China Sea. Before long, Madame Ching's Red Flag Fleet grew to two thousand ships and fifty thousand pirates and was feared from Hong Kong to Vietnam, the Chinese coast to Malaysia. Despite these impressive numbers, her greatest accomplishment was knowing when to quit. Out of desperation, the emperor granted amnesty to all of her pirates in 1810, along with the right to retain all of their plunder. Madame Ching was granted a command with the imperial fleet (assigned to her new husband), a palace, and high state honors for her and her captains.

carried a letter of marque, acquired by bribing high-ranking government officials, at various times from a variety of South American governments (Cartagena, for example), giving him a legal excuse for his piratical endeavors in the Gulf of Mexico during the early nineteenth century.

Unfortunately, many of our brethren only became the stuff of legend because they were killed in combat or captured and executed. In that respect, the most successful members of our ranks are those who somehow manage to avoid capture or killing and sail off into the sunset, able to live out the rest of their days enjoying the spoils of their piratical plunder. One of the few notable pirates to achieve this feat is Henry Every who, after making one final appearance on the island of New Providence, where he presented Governor Nicholas Trott with innumerable exotic gifts, disappeared from the history books. Then, the "Arch Pirate," who had just scored the biggest booty haul in piratical history—the capture of the *Ganj-i-Sawai*—disappeared without a trace, never to be heard from again.

But before a pirate will consider getting out of the game—assuming he isn't captured or killed long before the opportunity arises to make that decision—he will attempt to amass as much booty as possible. And while the vast majority of plunder comes from ships, more than a little bit also comes from land-based pillaging.

Demons on water, pirates are absolute hell on earth as well. We've ransacked and plundered innumerable hamlets, villages, towns, and cities over the years, causing many to seek protection from the military, or post lofty rewards for our capture and subsequent execution. But despite the dangers, we still go ashore quite often to raise Cain and have a little piratical fun.

Worth noting: Ransacked populaces don't just help individual pirates become rich. In some instances, plunder benefits an entire nation. For example, the Spanish robbed the Aztecs and Incas of their precious

HOT, COLD, LUKEWARM, IT DOESN'T MATTER HOW REVENGE IS SERVED—IT'S ALWAYS SWEET!

CAPTAIN BARTHOLOMEW "BLACK BART" ROBERTS was absolutely heartless in his treatment of sailors from Martinique and Barbados solely because the governors of those islands sought his capture. One of Black Bart's flags even depicted him standing on the skulls of the two governors. In one incident, the victims of a Martinique vessel were flogged, others had their ears cut off, and some were hung from the yardarms and used for target practice.

ANNE BONNY'S ESCAPE

ANNE BONNY was sentenced to be hanged along with "Calico Jack" Rackam and nine other members of the *William*'s crew. But because Bonny "pleaded her belly" (she was pregnant), she was spared from execution and jailed instead, only to somehow escape and disappear, never to be seen or heard from again.

[FIG. 38] PLEADING HER BELLY

treasures and then caravanned the booty across the Isthmus of Darien and onto the treasure fleets, thereby helping Spain become the wealthiest country in the world.

However, sometimes ransacking and pillaging is not the best way to find the booty. Valuables and treasure aren't always in plain view. And when the plunder is hidden, the most effective way to find it involves getting someone to talk. Unfortunately, cross looks and harsh words don't loosen lips. For those situations, fear, and if it comes to it, force, are necessary. Unfortunately, that means torture. But when it comes to getting our hands on gold, silver, jewels, and other valuables, believe me when I tell you we have absolutely no qualms dispensing pain in great quantities to find what we're looking for.

If after amassing your fortune, you've decided the dangerous seafaring trade is no longer in your bones—assuming you survive long enough to make that decision—becoming a broker of booty and plunder can be a lucrative career. Adam Baldridge, a veteran buccaneer himself, built a stone fortress with a battery of forty great guns protecting a bottlenecked harbor on the tiny island of St. Mary's, off the eastern shore of Madagascar. Here, he had reign over dozens of warehouses filled with pirate plunder, and acted as an agent for New York pirate broker Frederick Philipse. Some useful broker tips:

1. Location, location, location. Find an island or location along the seaboard where pirates can readily unload their booty (without fear of being caught) for barter, or at outrageous prices (in your favor, naturally). Pirates will gladly pay for what they want and need—if they can't steal it!

2. Remember the types of people you'd be dealing with. If they can't afford your exorbitant prices, or if they can't come to an agreement with your bartering terms, they may try to steal your goods—perhaps even killing you first—so have a dependable security force in place.

LIVE SOULS MAKE THE BEST BARGAINING CHIPS.

When **HENRY MORGAN** invaded Porto Bello in 1668, he used the women, old men, nuns, friars, and even the mayor as human shields for his buccaneers to storm the Santiago Castle. Ultimately, Morgan captured the city and demanded a 350,000-peso ransom or else he'd burn the city to the ground. Of course, they paid.

At the height of his piratical career, **BLACKBEARD** sailed directly into the port of Charleston (South Carolina) with his four-ship, 400-man pirate fleet and set up a blockade of the harbor. In one week he seized eight ships and kidnapped several prominent local citizens for ransom. All commerce to the large American seaport was curtailed, and the name of Blackbeard was forever etched into the annals of history.

TIGHT LIPS ARE FOR FOOLS. SOONER OR LATER, EVERYONE TALKS.

EDWARD ENGLAND was wise enough to know that dead men tell no tales. But that didn't mean he wouldn't scare the bejesus out of them to get them to talk. Upon capturing a merchant vessel, England would instruct his pirate crew to tie double-headed shot around the captive captain's neck and toss him overboard unless he revealed where the ship's valuables were hidden. If the merchant captain obliged, he was spared. If not, Davy Jones welcomed another eternal guest.

After a crewmember aboard the captured *William and Mary* was beaten, bound, and tied to the bowsprit, **CHARLES VANE** gave his pirate crew permission to place burning matches in the victim's eyes until he confessed what riches were aboard the ship.

ROGUE STRATEGY

How to Make and Use a Woodling Cord

This nasty torture device causes many a man to talk—and many others to wish they had!

1 **TIE** a pair of knots in the middle of a two-foot length of rope. Distance between knots should be the distance between the prisoner's eyes.

2 **TIE** ends of the rope into a secure knot.

3 **FORCE** prisoner to kneel, and bind his arms behind his back.

4 **PLACE** cord around the prisoner's head, with the two knots directly over his eyes.

5 **INSERT** a belaying pin or a one-foot length of wood between cord and the back of the prisoner's head.

6 **SLOWLY** twist wood in a clockwise direction, increasing pressure on the eye sockets via the knots.

7 **STAND** back. If the prisoner doesn't speak, his eyes might implode and squirt all sorts of nastiness on your feet.

CAPTAIN'S LOGBOOK

Our canoes returned on the 25th, who gave us an account they would pay no more than two and twenty thousand pieces of eight for the rest of the ransom, and that the tenient would pursue his Prince's orders, who forbade the payment of any more. That he had five thousand men at hand, with which he waited to see if we would put our threats in execution. Upon this fierce and bold answer, we had a consultation together, whether we should cut off the heads of all the prisoners. The plurity of voices, together with mine, was that it were better we should go and look after the two and twenty thousand pieces of eight, than shed any blood.

SIEUR RAVENEAU DE LUFFAN,
A Journal of a Voyage Made into the South Sea by the Freebooters of America (**1698**)

ISTHMUS OF DARIEN

Also known as the Isthmus of Panama, this narrow strip of land between the Pacific Ocean and the Caribbean Sea is both an important trade route and a fantastic short-cut between the two bodies of water. This is where **SIR FRANCIS DRAKE** ambushed and plundered the Spanish Silver Mule Train in 1573.

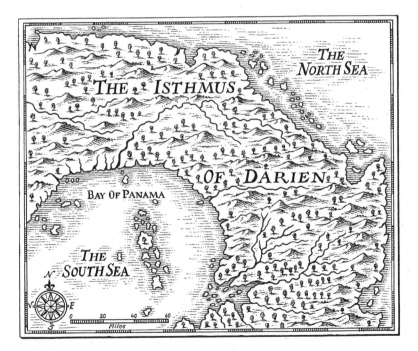

[FIG. 39] ISTHMUS OF DARIEN

They proceeded now to the West Indies, but before they had gotten far on their voyage, they attacked a rich Portuguese ship, called the Nostre Signora de Victoria, bound home from Bahia, and after some resistance, took her. *Edward Low* tortur'd several of the men, to make them declare where the money lay, and extorted by that means, a confession that the captain had, during the chase, hung out of the cabin window, a bag with 11,000 moidores, or which, as soon as he was taken, he cut the rope, and let it drop into the sea.

Low, upon hearing what a prize had escaped him, rav'd like a fury, swore a thousand oaths, and ordered the captain's lips to be cut off, which he broil'd before his face, and afterwards murdered him and all the crew, being thirty two persons.

CAPTAIN CHARLES JOHNSON,
A General History of the Pyrates (1726)

3. Even better, keep some pirates on your payroll. If pirates have plunder they aren't willing to part with for the deal you quoted, steal it from them. All is fair in business and piracy!

4. Develop a network of relationships that allow you to sell the contraband at inflated prices and purchase necessities on the cheap.

As you know by now, pirating is not for the squeamish. The lifestyle takes a serious toll on all who live it, and many a man who enters the profession does not last very long, for a wide variety of reasons. So when all is said and done, and your piratical run has finally come to an end, if you are still among the living and can manage a paper and quill, take the time to chronicle your exploits in the hopes that your legend will live on long after your bones have turned to dust.